Consensual Democracy

Consensual Democracy

Jay Wurts

First Published as www.ConsensualDemocracy.com under license by Creative Commons: 2009, 2012

eBook ISBN-13: 9781548710323
ISBN-10: 1548710326
Library of Congress Control Number: 2017910776
CreateSpace Independent Publishing Platform
North Charleston, South Carolina

Visit the author's website at www.JayWurts.com

Printed in the United States of America

Contents

Introduction: Democracy and DNA

THE THIRST FOR FREEDOM–for individualism within a social setting–is in our blood. It's a force of human nature as powerful as our urge to walk, to procreate, to explore and know the world. Much of human nature is self-interested, but that self-interest includes a desire to avoid domination while living harmoniously with others: to share autonomy and control at least the more important aspects of our lives.

Despite the claims of many politicians and bosses, most of us grow up to live our lives in a reasonably balanced and responsible way. After all, society is our natural environment. Collectively, we are the tissue of the human race. Developing in the womb, we mimic the evolution of our entire species: transforming ourselves from a single cell to an aquatic creature (complete with gills and vestigial tail) and finally a nursing mammal that, as soon as our wobbly legs can carry us, zooms off to explore the limits of our house, the city, and foreign lands. Some of us have even bathed in the light of alien worlds, and we're not about to stop there.

As we mature, our minds race to keep pace with our bodies' astonishing changes. Psychologically, we surrender our place at the center of a childish universe to reap the rewards of adult society. We learn that some kind of voluntary, reciprocal moral behavior is needed to keep that society together. We learn to compromise, collaborate, and delay gratification. We suppress much of the anger, fear, and pride that do not build strong individuals, but isolates them. Through education and experience, we become the sentient beings anticipated by our collective name: Homo sapiens.

And as we mature, our capacity for individual and collective action grows. We make mistakes, but we learn from them and build steadily on that knowledge. Ox-carts give way to automobiles, and kings are replaced by parliaments, but we don't stop after the first good symphony or vaccine. Each accomplishment only whets our appetite for more. If we can't achieve great things ourselves, we help those who do by raising children, paying taxes, giving to charities, voting, and volunteering. By adding our voice to the grand polyphony of life, we become not just the beneficiaries of progress, but its authors.

Most of all, learning to be human means learning to be free. The goal of this brief book is to show how our natural, biological drive toward physical and psychological maturity individually triggers our equivalent growth toward political and economic autonomy collectively. It shows how, despite periodic setbacks–both imposed and self-induced–our quest for personal and shared autonomy is on track. Freedom is more than a good idea: it's our genetic heritage. Exercising that freedom in the form of direct, consensual participation in the political and economic decisions that affect us most has been the goal of our eons-long experiments in self-governance. Achieving it in a practical, widespread, and sustainable way will be an evolutionary step as significant as the first human footprint on dry land or on the surface of the moon. The big idea here is that, left unimpeded, our destiny is to collaboratively control the conditions of our own existence. Here is a preview of those conditions necessary and sufficient to achieve that shared autonomy–ideas explored in this book. Consensual democracy requires us to:

> *Mandate consensus,* not win-lose contests. As we'll see, decisions arrived at through an iterative process of ever-widening stakeholder consent are qualitatively better and have lower cost of enforcement than decisions imposed by guardians–not just because fewer people oppose them, but because more people are committed to making them work. One-time, majority-rule contests produce winners and losers; and nobody likes to lose. Such contests decide everything and settle nothing. Decentralized information gathering, personal deliberation, and serial (and often multiple-choice) voting–all aimed at approaching consensus–lie at the heart of shared autonomy.

Emphasize contracts, not compulsion. By definition, contracts are voluntary, reciprocal, and based on informed consent. They contain duties, obligations, and the means to evaluate performance, enforce key provisions, and resolve disputes. By making the theoretical "social contract" between citizens and government more literal, we harness the power of voluntarism and reduce dependence on state coercion. By making the traditional "employment contract" more participative and extending it to all of a company's material stakeholders, we take corporate governance out of the hands of those who might abuse it and distribute it more fairly among all those contribute resources, leadership, inspiration and perspiration.

Reject involuntary hierarchies in favor of heterarchy. Human beings love all kinds of pecking orders, from those based on good looks and talent to wealth and useful skills. Good hierarchies turn bad when they become involuntary and coercive: roles become castes and mobility–upward, downward, and lateral–is constrained. Under heterarchy, society's major functions are coordinated by collaborative groups, not authoritarians, reducing opportunities for exploitation and abuse.

Create a culture of material stakeholders. People can't participate in every political and economic decision, at every time and place, and few would want to try. Instead, consensual democracy creates a fluid system in which participation is based on common sense, practical need, and individual capability and motivation. While we may all be stakeholders in all of society's functions, we are material stakeholders in a relative few–and that's where consensual participation begins.

Acquire the skills of shared autonomy. We are born with certain aptitudes–athletic, artistic, and otherwise–but they need cultivation to grow. More than anything else, consensual democracy means a lifelong commitment to the learning and teaching process: the more we participate, the better we do it–a skill we can share and pass on to later generations.

Substitute participation for representation whenever possible. Juries are a cornerstone of Western justice–and for good reason.

Some system of citizen jury-commissioners–people randomly selected from a pool of qualified candidates who are willing to serve for a limited time but cannot seek to join a specific jury-commission–will perform many functions now monopolized by well-insulated guardian elites.

Engage in political as well as economic "markets." In a consensual democracy, it should be no more difficult–or easy–to run for executive office or sponsor a ballot initiative than it is to start a business; and the degree of difficulty of that public action should be proportional to its social power or collective cost. Agenda-setting and decision-making at all levels are open to material stakeholders willing to devote the time and effort needed for meaningful participation.

Naturally, whole books could be written about any of these key principles. A brief work like this can only sketch a few good reasons why these factors are essential, but reason alone can't do the job. Overcoming our eons-old tradition of anti-democratic, guardian-based politics and economics can be achieved only by experience–through true education–not rhetoric. All a book like this can do is encourage guardians and their disciples to become skeptics and put their cherished assumptions to the test. Widespread consensual democracy is idealistic, to be sure, but no more so than guardianism's own starry-eyed premise: that a few privileged people are always more capable than the whole in determining the requirements for, then realizing, a good life. The real question is not one of idealism, but which ideals are worth pursuing, which have the fewest unintended bad consequences, and which bring out the best–and not the worst–in human nature.

Once our guardians and their boosters see that the world doesn't end when their circle of power expands to include the rest of us, a wealth of reasons will spontaneously appear for sustaining our experiment–just as arguments in favor of feudalism, mercantilism, slavery, and the divine right of kings all evaporated when more democratic systems took their place. Eventually, the day will come when we can conceive of no other way of living, and we will wonder why our ancestors put up with so much frustration, injustice, and waste for so long.

In a way, this book is a blueprint–an owner's manual–for a wondrous machine you've always possessed but seldom used. Its components have been tested by time, its design has been blessed by some of the world's best thinkers–but some assembly is required. That much-maligned and misunderstood advocate of practical government, Niccolo Machiavelli, said that to govern is to imagine; to make believe and make beliefs.[1] How much better our world will be when we imagine, then realize, institutions that promote the best in each of us.

Yet living free does not mean living without risk, even when following freedom's rule book. Consensual democracy in politics and economics is not about guaranteeing a desired outcome but about perfecting an essential process. The only outcome that is truly guaranteed by consensual democracy is the enhanced legitimacy of binding decisions and our greater commitment to making them work. To the degree that consent, not coercion, motivates us to obey our own rules, respect each other's rights, and preserve the natural world around us, the fruits of consensual democracy–of direct participation in the economic and political matters that affect us most–will include a better life.

---

1 Machiavelli, Niccolo. *The Prince*. Translated by Hill Thompson. New York: The Heritage Press. 1954.

1
Who Are Guardians and Do We Need Them?

PLATO BELIEVED the best societies were crafted by the best people. He wanted citizens of good birth to be selected at infancy and raised as philosopher kings. He called these special people *guardians*.[2]

He assumed that because of their superior qualities and education, they would pass good laws, administer justice fairly, and look after the lesser citizens around them.

In this book, we'll take Plato's lead and call a guardian anyone who acts in the name of, on behalf of, or in place of another citizen or group of citizens, whether or not it is with their consent.

This latter distinction–guardianism by custom or default, and not by choice–is not always obvious, but it's always significant. U.S. Congressional representatives, state legislators, and members of parliament, for example, are obviously guardians–we elect them for that purpose; but so is anyone who holds another person's "power of attorney," such as a relative making health-care decisions for a comatose loved one. On the other hand, guardian power does not extend to a lawyer representing a client in court. Although the lawyer is a "representative," he or she is told by the client how to plead, even in criminal cases where life or death is at stake. The client also makes all other major decisions about a case, such as whether or not to accept a proffered plea bargain or a settlement in a civil suit.

---

2 Plato. *The Republic*. New York: Penguin. 1974.

In all these instances, the people "guarded" have a say about who will make these important decisions or, in the lawyer-client relationship and when citizens vote on a ballot initiative, they can make such decisions themselves. But what about those guardians we never meet, choose, or know about, but whose decisions still control major aspects of our lives?

Economically, the executives and board of directors of a corporation act as guardians for the stakeholders in that company—not just share owners and employees, but also customers who rely on (and sometimes trust their lives to) product quality, families who depend on employee paychecks, and neighbors who must live with those guardians' decisions that result in noise, toxic waste, and traffic congestion. Similarly, the owners of real property (including proprietors of small businesses) are its guardians when it comes to determining its use and the disposition of its yield, regardless of the preferences of other stakeholders, such as tenants (who may make the property their home) or hired caretakers, who derive a living from its maintenance. Public statutes and business or environmental regulations—usually made by other guardians—may constrain or influence the actions of these decisionmakers, but it is the age-old laws and customs of property that make them platonic guardians.

This raises the crucial question of guardian functions versus guardian roles. A "guardian function" is merely stewardship. Every society must make practical choices—in general and in particular—about how to use its shared resources, how its citizens should behave, and how its rules should be enforced. Even in the most committed direct democracy, such as Athens in its Golden Age, not every citizen could have a meaningful say in all issues at all times, so key guardians—mostly executives—are selected to enforce the collective will. A "guardian role," however, is something else. It reflects the platonic belief that guardianship is, and must be, performed by exceptional individuals—whether those exceptional qualities are inbred, acquired through education, a gift of God, an aristocratic right, or imputed by popular election. A jury or commission can perform the guardian function very well, but only a professional politician or landlord or patriarchal chieftain can fulfill the platonic guardian role.

Guardian*ism*, therefore, is the philosophical belief that only one or a few people must control a society's resources and regulate the behavior of its members, with or without their consent.

At the extreme non-consensual end of guardianism are warlords who seize power and property at the point of a sword. Their strength, they claim, is all the proof they need of their superior status and justification to rule.

At the more participative end of the spectrum are elected representatives who operate within the framework of a constitution. They come into power "by the consent of the governed," as one historical document puts it, but that is the last time the governed need be consulted about anything. After election, representatives "represent" only themselves and are famously free to vote their own consciences–or anyone else's.

Thus despots and elected representatives form one continuous arc of guardianism, the difference (though the latter is certainly preferable to the former) being only one of degree. While elected legislators have more moral authority than military dictators, both maintain their special status, and perform the guardianship function, by excluding everyone else from setting agendas and making binding decisions, reserving those vital processes for themselves.

Although Plato never saw his ideal republic in action, his beliefs have appealed greatly to those who wish to rule and those who are willing to be ruled by others. What made the whole notion of guardianism–at its heart so undemocratic–so seductive?

Guardians and their boosters rest their system on three major premises: that ordinary people lack the capacity (training, experience, maturity, etc.) to self-govern; that superior people (guardians in the platonic sense) make consistently better decisions than ordinary citizens; and that a majority of ordinary citizens, if allowed to govern themselves, will tyrannize the minority. Although accepted as gospel by autocrats and democrats alike, none of these rationales hold water.

Despite age-old guardian assertions that direct democracy is social suicide, experience suggests otherwise. Ordinary people can–and do, when given the chance–manage their individual and joint affairs quite nicely, and without the power of the sheriff to compel obedience to their shared decisions. Even Montaigne, no particular friend of participation, observed that while "storming a breach, conducting an embassy, ruling a nation are glittering deeds," it is even more remarkable and difficult to "live together gently and justly with your household" and cited Aristotle (Nichomachian

Ethics) when he said that "private citizens serve virtue as highly and with as much difficulty as those who hold office."[3]

As it turns out, the vast majority of adults–all raised in a culture soaked in guardianism–conduct themselves as reasonable, responsible, and law-abiding citizens without a continual appeal to guardians. If they didn't, our economy would be in shambles (few people would hold jobs–why work when you can steal?–or voluntarily pay their bills and taxes); our cities, suburbs, and farms would be in ruins (why maintain property when any band of thugs can take it away?), and every street corner would be dominated by bullies. Certainly, there are exceptions to this age-old pattern, as when societies collapse after a war or when a repressive regime is removed, but these upheavals are usually guardian-induced, or follow the fall of an entrenched guardian class, only proving the rule.

The bottom line here is that while guardian functions like tending infrastructure, foreseeing and accommodating collective needs, and resolving conflicts between groups or individuals are essential, there is nothing essential about having them performed by guardians–at least in the platonic sense. Indeed, as we will see, the performance of these functions through self-selected guardians (yes, even elected guardians are self-selected: they must decide to run for office) often promotes the kinds of contention and disorder guardianism is supposed to prevent.

The second pillar of guardianism holds that one or a few superior (well-educated, mature, and highly trained) people will make better decisions about most things–especially important things–most of the time, and should therefore enjoy positions of authority over their less gifted fellows; but this, too, flunks the tests of both logic and experience.

First, unless the people fulfilling guardian roles are super-beings from some alien planet and are not derived from the demos (the politically active population), the abilities of the few can never exceed the aggregate abilities of everyone–a logical impossibility. That is, if guardians are drawn from the same population they govern, their knowledge, skills, and judgment in all areas cannot exceed the knowledge, skills, and judgment of the entire population, of which they are a part, when that population acts on

---

3 Montaigne, Michel de. Translated by M.A. Screech. *The Complete Essays*. London; Penguin Books. 1987. 912.

its own behalf. In fact, when guardians act in isolation, their abilities must necessarily be less. After all, no person is an expert in all things; and to become an expert in one or a few fields, it is necessary to forego education and experience in others. Further, part of becoming an expert is learning to view the world through an increasingly narrow focus, and this can lead to distorted perceptions–even arrogant disdain–for areas in which that expertise does not apply.

What guardians really mean when they say that ordinary people are not fit to govern themselves is that common citizens lack training and experience in guardianism–in mastering and exploiting a system that is designed to exclude others from sharing significant political and economic power and in brokering deals among that anointed few–and in this they are absolutely right.

The premise of the "flawed and unfit common man" is also refuted by statistics. Eighteenth-century philosopher and mathematician, the Marquis de Condorcet, offered quantitative proof that group-based decisions were usually superior to those arrived at by even highly qualified individuals.[4] He assumed that average citizens were reasonably intelligent, but not infallible. This meant that, in the long run, their common-sense decisions–about who is guilty of a crime, for example, or what crops to plant, or whether a new toll road or dam should be built–would turn out to be the best choice at least half the time: say, a bare minimum of 51-percent. (If it were otherwise, and people failed more often than they succeeded, civilization would have never have gotten off the ground and we would still be living in caves.) Under the laws of probability, he reasoned, the chance of a beneficial outcome increases in proportion to the number of citizens deciding the question. In a group of 100 citizens, for example, the probability that 51 (a bare majority) will arrive at the best decision is a modest 52 percent. If the majority rises to 55 citizens, however, the probability rises to 60 percent. With a majority of 60 people, the probability zooms to 70 percent–a remarkable and significant improvement.

Hence, Condorcet argued that the best possible choice depends not just on democratic action, but on creating the largest possible demos and

---

4 Dahl, Robert A. *Democracy and Its Critics*. New Haven: Yale University Press. 1989. 142.

striving for consensus. But his analysis didn't end there: as citizen education increased, so did the probability of their arriving at the best decision–and at a rate much faster than before. If education raised the average citizen's chance of making a good decision by a mere 4 percent–say, from 51 to 55 percent–the probability that the same bare majority (51 citizens out of 100) would arrive at the best decision soars to an amazing 60 percent. This doesn't mean that one or a few individuals couldn't make a decision of the same quality, only that there is no statistical inference that they would–and when the realities of guardian politics and the psychology of ambitious rulers are considered, good reason to suppose that they would not.

"Condorcet's Rule" seems to have been validated later by what became known as the "Flynn Effect," in which cumulative IQ scores during the twentieth century rose steadily as mass education took root in industrialized nations. Today, the average American's IQ score is equivalent to the top 2 percent of test-takers at the end of the 1800s–paralleling, coincidentally, the rise of, and demand for, direct citizen participation through state initiatives, referenda, and progressive management reforms that occurred during this same period.[5]

While Condorcet's Rule and the Flynn Effect make a powerful case for more democratic processes, they also draw attention to the so-called super-majority problem wherein a die-hard minority can frustrate the will of a large majority when such super-majorities are required, such as the two-thirds majority required for Congress to override a presidential veto. Such rules, while intended to maximize the chance for a good decision, paradoxically increase the chance of making a bad one, since they give disproportionate power to what is sometimes a less informed and intransigent few. As it turns out, the root of the super-majority problem has nothing to do with statistics, IQs, or the competence of those casting the votes but can be traced to our time-honored–yet very damaging and dangerous–system of one-time, win-lose, binary voting, a subject we'll examine shortly. Suffice it to say now that majority (or even super-majority) rule is not consensus; and when it is applied habitually in one-time, winner-take-all

---

5 Eliot, Lise. *What's Going On in There? How the Brain and Mind Develop in the First Five Years of Life.* New York: Bantam Books. 1999. 429.

contests of power, the results differ only slightly from decisions made by guardians to the exclusion of everyone else.

This leads us to the guardian's final argument for their own indispensability: the power of a citizen majority to oppress a minority.

Guardians love to equate mob rule with direct democracy, which is like comparing a street mugging to taxation. Both redistribute income but their processes are quite different, and neither mob action nor participation have anything to do with the power of an assertive majority–elected guardians or voters acting directly–to push around a minority. If a majority can pass laws to terrorize a minority, it makes no difference if that majority is comprised of elected representatives (a parliament, congress, or state legislature) or their constituents. What prevents any majority from abusing a minority is not guardianism but constitutional rights, procedural checks and balances, due process (in legislative as well as judicial functions), and the character of those who both make and live with the law–and these factors apply no matter how big the body of lawmakers gets.

In this regard, guardians forget that all the tools that help make representative government work are also available to help direct democracy succeed as well. As Robert Dahl reminds us, no legitimate government ever rightfully does everything it can do, any more than trustworthy police officers do all they might do simply because they have a badge and a gun.[6]

How, then, can we satisfy our need for guardian functions without surrendering ourselves to guardianism?

One answer lies in human nature.

Rousseau, one of the first modern champions of consent, wrote that we're born free yet find ourselves everywhere in chains.[7] Actually, the reverse is true. Human beings are born into abject dependence on a special set of guardians–our parents–then gradually outgrow our need for them. And what we experience individually, we yearn for collectively.

Parental substitutes–authority figures, rule-makers, and lawgivers of every kind, from teachers and police officers to bosses and bureaucrats– supervise each step of our journey to human maturity. They become our

---

6 Dahl. *Democracy and Its Critics.*

7 Rousseau, Jean-Jacques *The Social Contract.* New York: Hafner Publishing Co. 1947.

role models and, after we've achieved a degree of autonomy, many of us become guardians ourselves: business owners, executives, landlords, politicians, and of course, parents to children of our own. On the surface, this venerable cycle would seem to say something about the inevitability, if not desirability, of guardianism as a fundamental human institution; but again, habit does not always reflect necessity.

If we look at guardian roles as a hierarchy, with the most powerful guardians on top and the least powerful on the bottom, and accept both that guardians have guardians (every boss has a boss, even if it's a committee of other guardians) and that guardians in different areas must often cooperate to achieve their goals, then human nature is actually more closely aligned with networks than with guardianism. In other words, although hierarchies of some kind are inevitable in human society (we will always admire and voluntarily defer to people of extraordinary merit, for example), a hierarchy of guardians–an exclusive, compulsory power structure wherein a few are given license to coerce the many–seems nowhere explicit. Such hierarchies are a dominant group preference, and while they may appear all too often, there is no compelling biological or sociological need for them. In fact, a rational look at how human beings actually mature–individually and together–make such non-consensual hierarchies seem not only unjustified, but also counterproductive and foolish.

The reason guardianism continues into adulthood–as it has throughout history–seems twofold. First, as we mature, we progress from total dependence on parents to interdependence with peers. Some of these peers, through indoctrination or inclination, exploit our prior dependence by assuming the role of surrogate parents, then conning–or bullying–the rest of us into believing it is good and necessary. While no one doubts that children need guardians, the object of maturation is autonomy, including the ability to live cooperatively with others. If we allow certain peers to assume quasi-parental authority over us, it is not because nature selected them to be bosses and lawmakers and the rest of us to remain child-like dependents, but because those more aggressive and guileful peers found it advantageous, rewarding–and possible–to suppress our natural drive toward autonomy and turn it into a dormant trait. Social networks, including voluntary hierarchies based on merit, benefit everyone. Guardian domination of these networks co-opts their benefits and reserves them for an anointed few. In exchange, guardians promise us parental protection and the bliss of an eternal childhood–even though we long ago shed such illusions and have otherwise assumed the responsibilities of full-fledged adults.[8]

Second, because human beings are social animals, a big part of growing up means learning how to make semi-autonomous and interdependent relationships work. We become moral people because morality facilitates cooperation and helps us build useful, mutually beneficial networks. As infants, we learn that the "fixed acts"[9] rehearsed in the womb (a sucking reflex, for example, that allows us to nurse right after we're born) must be augmented by more reasoned behavior when we encounter the wills of others–such as playmates who want the same toy. This is not simply expedience; it reflects an instinct to observe, understand, and interact with our own kind. This instinct for autonomy within a social setting seems "hardwired" into the human brain and is activated by experience.[10]

The resulting childhood network–one still dominated by parents, but complemented now by a variety of peer relationships–becomes a system in which fairness and reciprocity means as much as selfishness and brute force. Eventually, as young adults, we realize that what began as a system of attitudes and behaviors rooted in selfishness has flowered into one that accommodates the shared interests of all. At some point, we see that these unofficial rules for living (what Oxford philosopher Derek Parfit calls, "common-sense morality"[11]), have certain universal qualities: that truth is better than falsehood, that honesty is better than deceit, that my right to swing my fist necessarily ends at your nose. We become moral creatures whose natural self-interest includes the reasonable interests of others. At that precise moment, we begin to shed our need for guardianism, yet

---

8 Television commentator and former presidential and congressional aid Chris Matthews wryly observes that because Democrats tend to espouse welfare and nurturing issues— ideas traditionally associated with motherhood—and Republicans emphasize more paternal issues like security and frugality, "We have a 'mommy' party and a 'daddy' party, each servicing its constituent voters." (Matthews, Chris. Now, *Let Me Tell You What I Really Think*. New York: The Free Press. 2001.)

9 Hobson, J. Allen, MD. *The Chemistry of Conscious States*. Boston: Little, Brown 1994.

10 Eliot. 300.

11 Parfit, Derek. *Reason and Persons*. Oxford: Clarendon Press. 1984.

guardians persist in our lives. This is not because we need guardians, but because guardians still need us.

In short, as we mature, the gratifications of childish tyranny and a desire to imitate our powerful parents give way to the larger rewards and subtler skills of reciprocity, self-restraint, and cooperation. We redefine right and wrong from idiosyncratic and selfish terms to those that promote individuality within a social setting. It is a leap to adulthood we make in the company of our peers, leaving behind only those who persist in childish dreams of centrality and pre-eminence: those, in other words, who yearn to be our guardians.

Is guardianism necessary? The answer is yes, but only for biological and emotional children. If we fail to establish guardian-free political and economic institutions as adults, it is because our natural growth toward shared autonomy was pruned before it bloomed, its function pre-empted by those who would forever be our parents.

2

A Brief History of Guardianism

ECONOMIST ROBERT HEILBRONER identified four types of societies—primitive, imperial, feudal, and capitalist—as stages upon which the forces of domination and participation struggled for ascendancy.[12] In each, guardians and dependents reached some kind of understanding, or accommodation, that tilted the balance of power: sometimes in favor of guardianism, sometimes in favor of participation, but generally advancing, at least a little, the cause of shared autonomy. From these accommodations—attempts by each side to preserve and expand its gains while minimizing the gains of the other—a set of ever-expanding "middle liberties" emerged. It is from these middle liberties, the things government neither encourages nor prohibits but that individuals have a right to pursue, that most social progress has come; and as these liberties expand, progress itself comes faster.

Primitive, or traditional, societies some of which exist today in developing parts of the world, openly extend the parent-child relationship to their political institutions. Tribal leaders assumed the absolute—and absolutely natural—despotic powers of a parent over a village, clan, or territory. Even in developed nations, we evoke memories of this fundamental, satisfying relationship when we refer to our country's "founding fathers" and when business executives talk about their "corporate families"—omitting the all-important fact that families aren't democracies. To the extent that

---

12 Heilbroner, Robert L. *The Nature and Logic of Capitalism*. New York: W.W. Norton & Co. 1985.

our position in such artificial families reinforces our psychological view of ourselves and supports our immediate need for community and security, including the satisfactions of dominating those below us in a guardian hierarchy, most of us go along with such fictions and call them good. Anthropologist Lionel Tiger thinks this natural moral instinct–to judge good or evil in terms of how well our artificial kinships function–was bred into us over hundreds of thousands of years when primitive societies were the norm.[13] Most guardians today knowingly or unknowingly tap its residual power to keep dependents in their place.

Imperial societies form when primitive societies bump into each other and need new myths to explain why "our" family is better than theirs and why those others are inferior, dangerous, or evil. Imperial hierarchies differ from traditional hierarchies the way sexual assault differs from marital intercourse; primitive guardians are like husbands and fathers; imperial guardians are like rakes and rapists. Both govern through outwardly similar acts, but the psychological conditions surrounding them are vastly different. Under imperialism, the dependent citizen's childlike obedience changes from an act of filial obligation to one motivated by fear or ambition. In primitive societies, dissenters (such as those wishing to usurp guardianism and participate directly in the major political and economic decisions facing the tribe) are usually punished by ostracism or exile and are forced to leave the "family." Under imperialism, dissent must be visibly (and often violently) crushed, because fictional kinship cannot be assumed. A wrathful parent-despot can be intimidating, but few are as dangerous as the empire that strikes back.

Eventually, imperial guardians warp the imaginary parent-child relationship so badly that it becomes open exploitation. Imperial guardians no longer pretend to be surrogate parents, but represent themselves as godly heroes: warlords and overlords who demand and receive imperial emoluments, such as semi-holy places to live and work (a palace, a parliament building, a White House) and bodyguards of their own choosing (traditionally, armed soldiers and secret police, but modern political parties accomplish many of the same functions)–and an artificial clan is formed.

---

13 Tiger, Lionel. *The Manufacture of Evil: Ethics, Evolution, and the Industrial System.* New York: Harper & Row. 1987.

Once accepted by citizen-dependents, imperial guardians–whether conquerors like the Caesars or a hereditary aristocracy like the British House of Lords, or an elected aristocracy like the U.S. Congress–become extraordinarily hard to remove, no matter how badly they rule. Eventually, citizens seeking to grow beyond childish dependency learn they must either devote themselves to "public life"–seek admission to the governing, guardian clan–or accept the middle liberties offered by private enterprise, which can eventually lead to high economic guardianship and considerable social clout.

This is the dichotomy Aristotle referred to when he declared that a citizen's world was divided into two halves: *societas*, those voluntary, cooperative, nonviolent (but often highly competitive) activities we now call economic; and *civitas*, or civic engagement. Seldom have the twain ever met, even in the democracy of ancient Athens, where the demos was confined to non-slave, property-holding, male citizens who passed laws for themselves, but every one else as well. Direct democracy in imperial Greece may not have been despotism, but it was guardianism for anyone not in the club.

Still, the accommodation reached between Greek guardians and the rest of the population established a few moral principles that advanced the cause of participation in later centuries.

First, it created a moral basis for suffrage: those most affected by a law ought to have a voice in framing and enacting it–although the size of that demos and the method of participation (direct or indirect, active or reactive) was open to negotiation. The second principle was that nation and state are not synonymous. "Nations" were and are amorphous things—an abstraction that includes certain groups with a common ethnic history, creed, and so on, while excluding others who do not share that history or those beliefs. States, on the other hands, were and are geographically particular. They contain the demos, no matter how it is defined, blur the distinctions among "nations" contained within its borders, and inescapably link property–the very land upon which its people live–to political power, and therefore to guardianism.

Nation-states, a fairly modern concept, combined the ideas of group identity, economic and political guardianism, and geographic particularity, and in doing so, created a host of complications. Not the least of these was the question of domain versus dominion: what rights–economic and political–adhere to citizens simply because of where they live, or the place in which they were born? Ancient, imperial Rome addressed this problem with a new accommodation. It invented the notion of open citizenship: the idea that anyone, even someone from a conquered territory, could become a member of the demos, not just those "born into the clan." This did more than just create another form of artificial kinship within the state; it signaled a fundamental turn in Western civilization–that citizenship and the right to participate, even to become a guardian, was not fixed and limited to existing members of the "family," but was mutable and expandable. It acknowledged that some form of implied, enforceable social contract existed between those who made the rules and those who were obliged to follow them.

Imperial societies turn feudal when their guardians begin to rely on reciprocity, as well as coercion, to keep their states intact. In the West, the moral authority and physical power of the declining Roman Empire was inherited by a variety of medieval kings, dukes, and princes, including officials of the Catholic Church. To use Aristotle's terms, *civitas* became the province of hereditary nobles and religious leaders while *societas* stayed where it had always been–among ordinary citizens who saw private enterprise as the only way to improve their lives. Eventually, this private power–the ability to claim as lawful property the surplus of economic transactions–was accumulated by an urban bourgeoisie, a new class of economic guardians who admired and wished to emulate the nobility. From this new "regime of capital," as Heilbroner calls it, wealthy citizens and industrious groups began to exert a great deal of social and political influence–mostly to buy or bribe special treatment for themselves.

This was the beginning of modern liberalism. It was a time when individual rights were negotiated between government guardians and economic guardians within a mutually accepted framework of common law and state power. Society was still divided between guardians and dependents, but dependents with special economic resources now enjoyed more political clout.

This new reciprocity, although of no direct benefit to most people (such as ordinary peasants), advanced the cause of democracy by acknowledging the interdependence between two guardian "regimes"–the regime of capital and the regime of politics–and created an environment in which *constitutions*, both written and unwritten, could flourish, a development of enormous consequence.

Traditionally, constitutions were unwritten social contracts that specified the general rules under which future conduct would take place and be judged. Under a constitution, laws could not be passed arbitrarily, at the whim of political guardians, but only within an agreed-upon framework that respected the rights of particular citizens–mostly economic guardians. For their part, economic guardians promised to behave in a way that would not destabilize the state, such as inciting peasants to revolt or neglecting to pay their taxes. Both sides agreed that coercion, or threats of force *between guardian classes* was to be avoided and would be used only as a last resort when other forms of dialog such as petitioning and lawsuits had failed. These practices were the ancestors of the civil codes we know today, and we must never forget that contracts, not just swords, helped forge the modern world.

However, this latest accommodation created new tensions as well as harmony among guardians. Eventually, the demand by economic guardians for more political clout and the need of political guardians to retain their monopoly on violence while enhancing national wealth, led to a fourth societal form, one which eventually integrated both political and economic hierarchies into a single guardian class: capitalism.

Capitalist guardianship had the paradoxical affect of both strengthening guardianism while at the same time promoting wider and deeper democracy. By blending two previously separate guardian elites–the regime of capital with the regime of politics–the schism between ordinary people and their hereditary or self-selected rulers was finally brought into stark relief. The lens for his great revelation was the ancient institution of property.

3

Guardians and Private Property: Domain Versus Dominion

ROUSSEAU THOUGHT HUMANITY'S downfall began not with Adam and Eve and a bite from that fabled apple, but with their descendants' claim that people could somehow own the land that produced the tree.

Voltaire, in particular, didn't like this critique of one of our oldest and most cherished institutions. He asked rhetorically if farmers who sow, reap, and protect their land are somehow less entitled to its fruit than neighbors who snooze under a branch then eat when an apple falls.[14] Adam Smith believed our natural acquisitiveness, though full of risks, was like a "divine hand" that shaped social progress while creating wealth. Jeremy Bentham agreed, noting that the happiness of all can result only through the pursuit of happiness by individuals: a crowd can't feel good about itself when too many of its members feel bad.

All of these fine thinkers believed that without individual rights to property and legal assurance that we can enjoy the product of our labor (including its surplus), citizens would have no incentive to work, save, and invest. John Locke was adamant on this last point, demolishing two of the most potent arguments used for centuries against full-blown capitalism: namely, that profit was immoral because it impoverished others; and that accumulating wealth was inefficient because it prevented goods–including

---

14 Havens, G. R. *Voltaire's Marginalia on the Pages of Rousseau.* New York: B. Franklin. 1971.

money–from being used by those who needed it more. Rejecting the first point, Locke said that landlords who enclose and cultivate land invariably increase its yield, creating more–not less–resources for the community. As to the second, he argued that by converting surplus goods to money, which cannot spoil, wealthy people actually minimize waste and help others become wealthy by investing in new enterprises.[15]

So who was right: Rousseau and his followers, from ascetic monks to Karl Marx, who saw individual guardianship over real property as a real vice; or were Locke, Bentham, Smith, and Voltaire aware of something these "communitarians" had missed?

If we view property–not just real estate, but any significant possession–as "territory" in the animal sense, then subtler arguments about "efficiency" and "waste" fade into the background and our instinct for acquisition comes into clearer focus. In nature, territory means security: a safe place to hunt, graze, and reproduce. One cannot acquire and exercise other forms of power (let alone achieve more exalted goals in art, literature, and philosophy), if one feels insecure. Further, human beings see benefits in any sort of surplus–not just satisfaction of our personal wants and needs, but a force that unifies and strengthens the community. Shortages, we know, set people against each other and tear communities apart. And spending money is a social activity involving buyers and sellers, producers and distributors, that reveals the status and prestige of all involved. Wealth in any form is nothing more than a potential to spend, and both wealthy people and their stakeholders (heirs, employees, suppliers, venture partners, tax collectors, and so on) use many of their waking hours planning how and when such spending, including investing, should take place. Just as our ancestors depended on game-rich forests and fruited plains to keep their tribes safe and prosperous, so we depend on a growing stock of money–and on economically significant legal rights–for our security. Today, the political economy, that confluence between the regime of capital and the regime of politics we call a modern liberal capitalist republic, is the "natural" environment we must master in order to survive.

Because of that, all civilized societies implicitly or explicitly link property to power. In 1787, Noah Webster went so far as to say, "In what then

---

15 Heilbroner, *Nature and Logic of Capitalism.* 112-113.

does real power consist? The answer is short and plain–in property... A general and tolerably equal distribution of landed property is the whole basis of national freedom."[16] This connection was especially true in feudal and Renaissance societies, where political stability often depended on alliances among landed families and their cooperation with the minor nobility, tradesmen, merchants, and peasants who cleared, improved, worked, and defended new territory. Together, their efforts converted patchworks of farms and villages into networks of grand estates and cities served by roads, bridges, canals, aqueducts, and harbors–the infrastructure that tangibly linked individual well-being to the common good.

Large-scale capitalism made these long-established, cooperative relationships more efficient and created new forms of wealth, new guardian hierarchies, and new ways for individuals of all types, including non-propertied citizens, to advance their interests. But the underlying value of property–that sense of territory and our primeval attachment to it, including our necessary and useful feelings of patriotism toward our geographically defined nation-state–was the glue that held everything together. It was also a bomb that threatened, at regular intervals, to blow everything apart.

Just as political guardians could expropriate land and tax the wealth it produced under the principle of sovereignty, so did economic guardians expropriate the surplus generated by labor and trade under the rubric of traditional property rights. The conflicting moral claims to that surplus– who *should* control it: the tribe or the tribal chieftain? the provider of the tools or the one who uses them?–has been hotly debated ever since.

One way guardians accommodated these differences, though never completely resolving them, was to separate the *benefits* of property from its ownership. After all, land in any historical era, under any form of government, must be worked by somebody; and because citizens exploiting the land must be induced to labor upon it–often under bitter or risky circumstances—even the most distant and selfish landlords found it wise to grant certain benefits and prerogatives to those who actually occupied and developed the land. Thus, the clear, theoretical distinctions Rousseau,

---

16 Bailyn. *The Debate on the Constitution, Part 1.* 155, 158.

Voltaire, Smith, Locke, and others made about the morality of land ownership became muddied in actual practice.

Laws protecting rights in property–intended originally as an accommodation between political and economic guardians–later came to protect the interests of more modest and even non-propertied citizens. Indeed, as Ronald Dworkin observes, the U.S. Constitution intentionally strengthened the rights of private property-owners *specifically* to counterbalance the power of the state and reduce, as Madison put it, the "dangers of faction."[17] Unfortunately, those factions formed anyway, and property rights (and the other rights derived from them) usually were, and still are, at the center of their conflicts.

Among the earliest beneficiaries of these "fictitious" property rights were non-landed gentry, such as merchants, bankers, and investors who, although lacking the huge agricultural estates that characterized the feudal nobility, created great wealth by exploiting their knowledge of technology, trade, and finance. This minor gentry gradually became the professional and middle class that informed much of our contemporary, consumer culture. With this expanding base of economic guardians, the profit motive–the will to increase and expropriate surplus–received new moral justification and increased political clout. Profit was seen as society's, and God's, reward for individuals who were thrifty and satisfied their fellow citizens' wants and needs. It was also fair compensation for investors who risked money by subsidizing new ventures; and the riskier the venture, the greater the reward they deserved.

Without doubt, there is a compelling logic behind this. If income doesn't exceed expenses, there is no profit; therefore producers are motivated to preserve assets and keep waste to a minimum–although they are also motivated to charge the highest prices they can. This ability to decouple price from cost, to continue charging high prices even when costs and risks have diminished, has caused no end of problems in developed societies. It did not take much time for political and economic guardians to notice that by cooperating with each other, they could manipulate markets, exclude competition, raise and sustain high prices, and reduce

---

17 Dworkin, Ronald. *Freedom's Law: The Moral Reading of the American Constitution.* Cambridge, Mass.: Harvard University Press. 1996.

their dependence on thrift. Proprietors who founded big businesses, often experts in certain fields of production, discovered they could hire professional managers to "extract" surplus from material and human resources and thereby remove themselves from the cares and commitments of day-to-day guardianship. A nominal owner could now enjoy all the benefits of property without becoming embroiled in, or too empathetic with, the practical or moral problems of production. For example, the fragmenting of tasks that boosted efficiency by keeping workers focused on one part of the overall job, wound up limiting employees' interest in the company and their pride in the final product. Similarly, managers who monopolized the planning function taught citizen-workers to leave agenda-setting to others: an anti-democratic reflex political guardians were happy to encourage. Even worse, these developments led economic guardians to view employees as interchangeable parts in the vast machinery of production; and when technology or market conditions changed, disposable parts as well.

In the same vein, political guardians reconciled their often-conflicting duties to both worker-dependents and owner-guardians by sanctifying profit–which, after all, was the government's main source of revenue, through taxation. This led to a greater symbiosis between political and economic guardians, so that by the late nineteenth and early twentieth centuries, the regime of capital and the regime of politics had become virtually indistinguishable.[18]

However, predictable profits depend on public order, and there were practical limits to the accommodations political guardians could offer their economic counterparts. Disputes arose over what, exactly, constituted labor exploitation and market manipulation. Worker-dependents became more antagonistic and wary and sought relief by appealing to political guardians. Unions formed and lawmakers found themselves obliged to create whole new volumes of law aimed at solving problems that rarely existed in pre-capitalist days or had been handled through the surrogate kinships of paternalistic firms and landlords. Goodwill and community spirit–even common sense–diminished as aggrieved workers and managers, capitalists and politicians, became more confrontational and litigious. In both input (labor) and output (commodity) markets,

---

18 Heilbroner. *Nature and Logic.*

dog-eat-dog competition, economic predation, exploitation, and even sabotage became the order of the day.

Over time, these adversarial relationships created a division of *responsibility*, as well as a division of labor, in the political economy. As profit needed less moral justification (legality being the only real criterion), the burden of enforcing moral behavior shifted away from private citizens, including property owners–the "lord of the manor" being the traditional arbiter of village mores–and fell to political guardians. Under pressure from constituents and being excused from the risks of economic Darwinism, political guardians began pursing a more openly moral agenda. This didn't mean that public officials became more ethical or that better laws necessarily passed only that politicians had to *appear* to be addressing the worst abuses and immoralities of the marketplace in order to gain and keep their offices.

Of course, we must not conclude from this that capitalism and mass production are inherently evil or less democratic than other forms of political economy. Pre-industrial, cottage industries could be as chauvinistic, paternalistic, and exploitative (especially to women and children) as more centralized forms of production. The real villain in the industrial revolution wasn't manufacturing technology, or even the amoral wave of Tayloresque "human engineering" that followed it, but the extension of feudal property laws into new, non-feudal relationships that turned tenant-farmers into proletarians and successful proprietors into quasi public guardians with considerable–and usually non-consensual–social power.

Recall that territory–a simple geographic boundary–is used by all states to define their citizenship. With citizenship come specific burdens, such as involuntary taxation and compulsory military service, among others; as well as certain rights and benefits. Moral problems arise, though, when the specific parcel of land defining citizenship and creating those obligations (in other words, a citizen's domicile), is owned by someone else: not the citizen, but a private guardian, a landlord, or a corporation. What is the moral justification, critics ask, for compelling renters to pay their landlord's property-related expenses (such as mortgages and taxes) *and* risk their lives defending that property from harm (via conscription) while those same renters share few or none of the political and economic benefits of property guardianship?

This may seem like a trivial philosophical question, but the problem of landless, and often alienated, citizens has been a perpetual issue throughout history; and modern liberal capitalist representative democracies have done little—other than promote the distraction of consumerism and offer a few token reforms (in America, these include the G.I. Bill, FHA, and a mortgage aftermarket that facilitates home loans)—to address it.

Ancient societies like Greece and Rome were at least honest, if unegalitarian, about the problem of citizen-tenants. They simply declared landless people to be second-class citizens and assigned them a different set of civil rights and obligations, distinguishing legally and socially among different levels of wealth. For example, in the early Roman Republic, only landowners could serve in the army, since political guardians figured they had the most to lose in war. When these societies turned imperial, military ranks were opened to non-propertied citizens who enlisted with the hope of earning wealth (in the form of booty) and a grant of farmland promised by the state. Equality in those days wasn't a right: it was a reward that had to be earned.

Today, we offer our landless citizens no such options. Even renters who are veterans, discharged soldiers who risked life and limb defending national interests receive only modest discounts on home financing: their chance to become, in one small way, property guardians themselves. The resulting, de facto second-class status of landless citizens is potentially so dangerous and destabilizing that guardians no longer even suggest that land ownership and citizenship might somehow be connected. Instead, non-guardian renters are placated with surrogate rights derived from the property rights of guardians, typically in the form of "consumer rights" and legislation giving designated groups special protections, leaving the unique benefits of property owners relatively undisturbed. This is certainly an improvement over the bad old days of lordly estates and tenant-farmers' *rights in common* (although the king and parliament, not the people, still determined which land was public); but it's a far cry from the political economy self-governing people deserve.

In any event, in most states, residents are considered citizens—and thereby subject to all its laws, democratically made or not—when they are born into its territory, or to parents who were, or when they reside within its boundaries for a certain length of time and pass other tests for naturalization. Yet these citizens have no reciprocal claim against the land, or its yield, that created this obligation; nor do they have any particular, *personal* ties to their fellow citizens except their obedience to the rules imposed on them by guardians. This clause in the modern social contract is, by any objective standard, adhesive; and, if it wasn't for the principle of sovereignty, it would be unenforceable in any court. To the degree that practical power in such states resides with guardians, not the demos, this one-way arrangement would seem to be a misuse of the sovereign principle, which in modern times assumes that ultimate power rests with the people, not their agents. To the extent that economic and political guardians abuse this power, it is tyrannical as well.

Of course, some will argue that the state compensates for this ancient inequity by providing every citizen, landed or not, with police, fire, and military protection, a justice system, an infrastructure of roads and sewers, and so on. But on a case-by-case basis (which is the only way contracts–even social contracts–can be evaluated), state guardians often exempt themselves from the same responsibilities they demand of private citizens. For example, congressional representatives exclude themselves from Social Security taxation while requiring it from everyone else; and while police offer protection to the general public, they may deny it to any particular person except under special circumstances, such as witness protection and police bodyguards for public officials. (Call 911 if you're in trouble, and the police will eventually respond, but neither the city nor its agents are responsible if you are victimized by the time they get there.) And who can deny that the courts, including the criminal justice system, serve best those who are best connected? Even in the military, rent-paying Americans are far more likely to find themselves defending a landlord's property from a domestic riot, or advancing corporate guardians' interests abroad, than protecting their own family and neighbors from rapacious foreign invaders.

The point is, rent has always been a symbol for the alienation of landless citizens: a barrier between a large class of people and the state that claims their loyalty, lives, and taxes. It is a special problem for any society that espouses consent and democratic ideals while tolerating guardian authority.

This brings us back to another principle laid down by America's founders and articulated succinctly by John Jay: "The people who own the country ought to govern it." The question is: in a democracy of any kind, who rightfully owns the country?

4
Guardianism, Equality, and Fairness

DESPITE THE PROBLEMS created by guardian domination of property, the industrial revolution produced one of the most democratic innovations of all time: the joint stock company.

Early in the industrial revolution, when there were more new ventures than wealthy patrons to back them, entrepreneurs sought alternative ways to raise money. With the creation of joint stock companies, whose shares even people of modest means could afford, the benefits of property ownership became available to previously un-propertied citizens. If the venture succeeded, its share price increased and investors could sell their stock for a profit. To give these arm's-length investors at least a nominal says in the firm's activities, each share brought with it one vote on issues referred to shareholders by the company's primary guardians: its elected board of directors. Stockholders also enjoyed a claim against the firm's assets if the company went bankrupt (although their claim was subordinated to that of lenders) and received dividends, if the directors declared them, in proportion to their number of shares. It was plutocracy, not democracy, but it was more participatory than other forms of guardian ownership and established a principle of informed consent that continues to transform the political economy.

When attempts at property reform cut too close to private guardian interests, joint stock companies were incorporated or turned into a fictitious artificial person. This gave corporations many of the same rights and legal protections afforded to individuals. While there is no compelling social or economic reason to do this, there is a powerful legal and political incentive. By turning their companies into fictitious citizens, corporate guardians insulate their enterprises from unwanted intrusion by either the state or ordinary citizens while enjoying all the liberties designed to encourage individual civic participation–including the right to contribute money to candidates and lobby for specific legislation.

The success of this strategy, which took root in the nineteenth century and flowered in the twentieth, was not lost on other groups, particularly non-guardian activists weary of depending on guardian goodwill to achieve their aims. Just as individual rights were hijacked, so to speak, to benefit corporations, so were they co-opted by identity groups claiming rights parallel or superior to those of the general population. Using judicial activism to expedite or avoid the often lengthy and contentious legislative process, these groups advanced a wide range of programs in matters related to the environment, racial and gender discrimination, workplace and product safety–including special treatment for preferred groups, such as affirmative action–all under the banner of protecting individual rights.

These efforts, like economic guardians' efforts to protect and enhance the power of corporations, succeeded not because of any formal consensus within the demos, but because their sponsors were able to obtain at least a momentary choke-hold on the apparatus of legislation and judicial review. Unfortunately, even if one applauds their objectives, their methods devalued the idea of a uniform code of civil rights until today, issues involving the general will and common good rarely receive a hearing. Indeed, some guardians deny such things even exist; and if they exist, they cannot be knowable.

Key players in this undemocratic process are the public bureaucracies and private organizations established to implement guardian designs. In the public sector, state bureaucracy has become a virtual fourth branch of government, using its own weight, inertia, and regulatory and enforcement powers, as well as its independent legal resources, to exercise its (sometimes very independent) judgment and minimize outside interference–even by elected officials. In the private sector, advocacy groups and lobbyists perform what was originally conceived as the duty and prerogatives of individual voters: the "town hall" advisement of government officials. This led to another accommodation between elected and non-elected guardians as binding as any of history's other unwritten constitutions, the inviolability and indispensability of organizational, as opposed to individual, agency.

Temporary measures, such as the New Deal's efforts to mitigate the effects of the world wide Great Depression, not only amplified the power of bureaucratic guardians, it made them a permanent fixture in the political economy. Compensation due to loss or misfortune became not just one-time remedies for victims of droughts, floods, wars, and other disasters, but ongoing entitlements claimed by anyone who could show membership in a government designated, preferred group, including favored industries who received generous subsidies and tax breaks. In the latter half of the twentieth century, transfer payments to, and special considerations for, such groups were viewed as a property right, as sacred to those receiving them as any other constitutional guarantee. This led to a further accommodation between private and public guardians, transcending the ideology of the left or the right. The shared agenda of both liberals and conservatives–using the coercive power of the state to protect and promote the interests of favored groups–employed civil (including corporate) rights as bargaining chips. Each cycle of expanded individual rights created new privileged groups and, as the tension between majority rule and minority rights increased, governance (as James MacGregor Burns aptly puts it) by "stalemate and spasm."[19]

In short, so effective had the U.S. Constitution, as amended, been at forestalling the tyranny of the majority, that it had inadvertently created a tyranny of minorities–an all-but-official denial that anything remotely resembling the common good and general will could even exist.

The rallying cry for these special groups was perceived inequalities of all kinds, a traditional magnet for social theorists drawn to "first causes." Rousseau, for one, posited three stages of gradually increasing inequality, beginning with laws that made artificial distinctions among people (creating class); then progressing to institutions that enforced these class distinctions (discrimination); and culminating in groups that learned to monopolize political and economic power to keep their own guardians

---

19 Burns, James MacGregor, with Overby, L. Marvin. *Cobblestone Leadership: Majority Rule, Minority Power*. Oklahoma City: University of Oklahoma Press. 1990.

in control (tyranny).[20] He concluded, like Jefferson, that periodic revolutions were required to restore more equitable conditions once an intolerable level of inequality had been reached. Unlike Jefferson, however, Rousseau believed that strong democracy could not exist without checks and balances on the ownership and control of private property, which he felt was the root of most evil. This goes a long way toward explaining why political guardians on both the left and right bitterly resist any serious attempts to reform our fundamental modes of property ownership and control; a problem that is solved ceases to be an issue, or a rallying cry, and leaders require followers, guardians require dependents.

Nonetheless, inequality to some degree has always been the lifeblood of free enterprise. In the Middle Ages and Renaissance, successful merchants, craftsmen-inventors, and investment bankers seeking to improve their lot quickly became islands of prosperity in the feudal sea of manorial and ecclesiastical hierarchy. Roman law and Germanic custom reinforced an individual's claim to land, chattels, and labor, creating a robust system in which inequalities in one area were often counterbalanced by inequalities in another: what a rich man lacked in political clout, he made up for by exploiting his tenants and workers. Thus, Western political and economic institutions—spurred by technical advancements, discovery, and warfare—created a new kind of imperialism that converted "hit-and-loot" conquest to "grab-and-hold" colonization that depended as much on assimilation as suppression to control the local inhabitants.

When inequalities between segments of society, whether among various types of guardians or between guardians and dependents, get too great, pressure mounts for accommodation: restructuring of property laws or reapportioning of rights. When these accommodations fail, the stability of the state is threatened. From this perspective, the American revolution was more about adjusting marginal inequalities among guardians—substituting one form of representative guardianism in place of another—than about creating a free and equal new state for all. The French and Russian revolutions were more far-reaching, discarding "ancient regimes" for new ways

---

20 Rousseau, Jean-Jacques, trans. by Cranston, Maurice. *A Discourse on Inequality.* Middlesex: Penguin. 1984.

of defining social relationships, although those relationships, too, quickly became guardian-dominated and showed their anti-democratic colors.

The real question is not whether inequality is good or bad, but rather how much of it is fair. To answer this question, Robert Dahl suggests that three kinds of equality are necessary in a democracy.

The first is moral equality: all citizens are moral agents responsible for their actions. The second is personal autonomy: no citizen can dictate the conditions of another citizen's life. The last is political equality, best embodied in the ideals of "one citizen, one vote" and "equal treatment under the law."[21] Unfortunately, equal treatment under the law is often sacrificed in our relentless pursuit of the other two forms of equality: compensating people handicapped by nature, events, or their own bad decisions by giving them benefits not available to the general public; and mitigating guardian abuses by creating new guardian roles–leading mostly to new inequalities. We diminish legal equality whenever we use coercive state power to achieve one group's ends at the expense of another's, or when we let guardians use their own moral and economic preferences to make decisions for us.

In other words, equality turns out to be more meaningful as a journey than a destination: a moving target fixed by consensus, and adjusted periodically, not a static condition defined by guardians.

Over time, our tolerance for economic inequality increases our demand for political equality. The kind of inequalities we accept, however, tend also to complement and perpetuate the power of guardians who serve our interests. For example, on the pretext of defending individual or group rights, certain guardians regularly trample not only on the rights of out-of-favor groups, but diminish the value of universal rights–those used to pursue the common good and general will–possessed by the entire demos. Although we don't complain when our group benefits from this discrimination, it is hard to find a scenario–theoretical or otherwise–in which this condition meets the test of consensual fairness.

Consensual fairness in this sense may be defined as *the principle that makes any system of property, rights, and inequality acceptable to the demos.* The key phrase here is "acceptable to the demos"–not, "acceptable to

---

21 Dahl. *Democracy and Its Critics.*

guardians" or "acceptable to guardians acting on behalf of the demos," or "acceptable to those less fortunate," or "acceptable to those who are highly altruistic." Unfortunately, fairness is often depicted as being so subjective, relative, and situational that it defies description, let alone political or economic expression. It's better, most guardians think, to simply assume that fairness resides with them–as duly elected (or self-appointed) members of the power elite; or that fairness is a quality inherent in a particular set of beliefs, such as those reflected by a political party, a religion, or a set of corporate policies. Other utilitarians ask: why be fair at all? What's the point of moral behavior if immorality or amorality advances your cause and keeps you and your group in power? Such beliefs, obviously, lie at the root of much political and economic behavior, even when it is not articulated.

One problem all guardians face is that people, individually and in groups, have a real thirst for fairness and a good, intuitive sense of what it means. This quality is so pervasive in human nature that it seems to be an inextricable part of our mind-brain function, like our desire for autonomy. Without some innate and shared sense that "fairness counts," we would have no reason to maintain voluntary, reciprocal associations or resolve disputes nonviolently. We value fairness because, like Gordon Gecko's greed,[22] it works–and in the long-term, if not always the short. Unlike greed, though, we need no special argument to justify being fair. Any school child can give you a serviceable definition of what fairness is, and what we learn on the playground, we put to work later in boardrooms and at the ballot box.

Fairness at this intuitive level–what some call the Golden Rule of Equity–means that everyone gets more or less the same thing, or the same kind of treatment, unless they deserve something different. The real debate, then, is not the idea of fairness, but the definition of "deserving"– in other words, the meaning of *justice* in a given society.

---

22 A fictional corporate raider in Oliver Stone's 1987 film *Wall Street*, Gecko defended predatory capitalism with the catchphrase, "Greed, for lack of a btter word, is good. Greed is right. Greed works."–although he later expanded his definition to include not just acquisitiveness, but any form of ambition, including scientific curiosity and artistic creativity.

The sad fact is, equity does not always mean equality, and justice often demands that they be different. Guardians try to convince dependents that the inequalities resulting from their decisions are always just–a fiction necessary to preserve the status quo, if not their jobs. If guardians suggest that a given balance between equity and equality is unjust, it is usually because they are preparing to redistribute property or rights in favor of some newly preferred group so that, after the change is made, a critical mass of citizens will still feel comfortable with the accommodation. Because most guardians realize that coercive force usually causes a backlash, they seldom do all they can do for favored individuals or groups, but only as much as they can justify as "fair" at a given moment. When such changes are introduced incrementally over many years–as a "moving peg" upon which constituents may hang their day-to-day sense of equity— changes that society might have rejected outright or resisted bitterly are gradually accepted as just and fair.

For example, FDR's New Deal legislation was passed only after long and harsh debate and was struck down, in its earliest forms, as unconstitutional by the U.S. Supreme Court; whereas decades later, similar legislation–much of it going well beyond New Deal principles–passed Congress and state legislatures, not to mention judicial review, with relative ease. Similarly, objectives of the civil rights movement, which before 1964 demanded "equal treatment for all," had changed by the 1970s to "preferential treatment for some." Had Americans during these periods somehow changed their minds about what was fair and just? Or had guardians, in cooperation with preferred groups, gradually altered the terms of public debate so that the rights in question could be redistributed without causing excessive social disruption? Again, the question here is not the merits of any specific social proposal, but rather *whose* sense of justice does it serve? Just as a judge may not hear his own case, one aggrieved party ought not to be allowed to dictate the terms of a remedy to its opponents simply because it controls, however briefly, the levers of guardian power.

In the private sector, our sense of fairness is just as acute, but also subject to guardian influence. Employees know they sell their time and expend physical and mental energy at guardian direction, getting wages and benefits in return. Executives are often paid for results, not just effort, so their interests tend to be aligned more with owners than with the workers they manage—although this is not always the case. Because they have little control over how the money they provide is used, lenders and investors are given property rights that are legally and morally superior to the rights of other parties in a business. Generally, though, *all* participants claim their highest rewards and entitlements are fair—in proportion to the contribution they make to the enterprise, just as other stakeholders (customers, suppliers, politicians, and the local community) feel it is fair for them to have a strong voice in how the firm does business.

In fact, all these claims have merit. They go awry only when one group says its claims are more central to economic processes than all the others, all the time, and therefore deserve permanent preferential treatment. The point these adversarial stakeholders miss is that a political economy depends on all its parts. Non-consensual subordination of any one group to another cannot be justified by intuition or rational argument, or even an appeal to some abstract principle, but only by custom, tradition, bargaining, or coercive power. Since that's the case, the only people who can decide which stakeholder (or stakeholder group) should enjoy preference over another at any given moment are the stakeholders themselves, acting jointly, and not through power-wielding guardians allied with one particular group.

This model extends to the public sector. Political guardians, like everyone else, keep their own scorecard about who contributes what to society, to the party, and to each politician's career. This means public guardians have a pretty good idea about which individuals or groups should be rewarded or punished at any given time. Their priority is usually to reward first those who have helped them in the past, then reward those who can help them in the future—but practical reciprocity like this does not preclude altruism, or even a larger sense of justice. Although most public guardians act undemocratically, that by itself does not prevent them from being fair, public-spirited, and conscientious. Political guardians thus compare their personal contributions to society (and the psychic and material rewards they receive from them) to the contributions and rewards of other guardians, as well as those derived from, and bestowed upon, the dependents they represent. Just as economic guardians use property and profit as a measure of, and tool for, power; so do political guardians use rights and inequalities to reward and punish, to measure their own success, and to stay in power.

Thus begins a complex dance in which guardians measure each other's performance and worth, then invest, or disinvest, in each other's interests and careers. Here's how it works:

If an economic or political situation is truly unfair and the individual or group seeking redress is part of, or necessary to, the guardian's power structure, the changes the guardian proposes will be real. Such changes typically include a redistribution of rights or an increase, or decrease, in inequality in some area–usually through transfer payments, tax credits and deductions, the awarding of government contracts, or legislation that restricts or enables some type of economic or social activity.

If the situation is truly unfair but the individual or group seeking redress is not part of the guardian's power structure, or necessary to it, the change will be cosmetic or illusory. The tools of political illusion are vast; examples include nominal or hortatory resolutions, proposing bills that guardians know will fail in committee or flunk judicial review, and show-case legislation that placates critics while evading crucial issues.

Political guardians wield these two forms of power simultaneously–sometimes in the same piece of legislation, as when a law dealing with substantive matters contains a rider catering to some frivolous or pork-barrel issue. When such actions are linked to the parallel and equally self-serving activities of economic guardians, we get a society in which officially sanctioned rewards and punishments are notably different from those which make the political economy run most efficiently, effectively, and fairly. "Fairness" in this case becomes anything you can get away with: from golden parachutes for executives to brazenly illegal fund-raising by political candidates.

This brings us back to the original question, expressed in a slightly different way: Is it fair to use state power to make some groups or individuals better off while making other groups or individuals worse off, especially when guardians (by virtue of their monopoly over resources, agenda-setting, decision-making, and enforcement), have so much power to manipulate our perceptions? Even if the answer is yes, we may reasonably ask if it is fair to redistribute property and rights, or to increase or decrease inequalities, without the consent of those who must live with the consequences.

The ultimate answer, again, lies in defining fairness not as an outcome, but a procedure: a process for making decisions that is widely accessible and widely accepted. Because the particulars of every legislative bill or judicial verdict can't please everyone, and because some political and economic decisions will always cause more problems than they solve, the process by which these decisions are made must be accepted as valid, or even good laws and just verdicts will be rejected. A system that depends entirely on an unbroken string of successes for its politics can never last, because human beings make mistakes. A system that has the mechanism to detect and correct its mistakes, however, will likely stand the test of time. An unjust decision can result from a fair process and still be accepted by citizens (as, some will argue, was the case in the notorious O.J. Simpson criminal verdict or the controversial election of President George W. Bush in the year 2000); but people—especially those on the losing side—will never accept as just an adverse decision that resulted from an obviously unfair process: as asserted by many Japanese-Americans who were interned during World War II by federal edict without individual due process.

Bentham believed that the fundamental measure of a fair society was the broadness of its electoral base: the wider and deeper the demos, the more valid its laws become. By this reasoning, the mini-democracy called the U.S. Congress is about 500 times more valid and just than the rule of a single king; but even that system is about 500,000 times less valid and just than it would be if all Americans ruled themselves.

5

The Myth of Majority Rule

UNDER REPRESENTATIVE DEMOCRACY, or rule by elected guardians, collective decisions are binary: we vote or we don't, we vote for or against someone or something, we win or we lose. While nothing in the theory of representation, let alone democracy, requires this binary method, the adversarial mindset it creates (heartily endorsed by guardians and others who yearn for quick decisions) has made one-time, majority-rule ballots the *sine qua non* of democracy. We've been trained from childhood to see all conflicts as contests and because under guardianism the reins of power are destined always to be held by a few, we choose (to invert James Madison's famous dictum) "to indulge our fears rather than our hopes" and stake everything on these periodic bouts of ballot roulette.

In fact, history and psychology give us three compelling reasons to think that voting as a one-time, win-lose, majority-rule contest between two predetermined choices is probably the *worst* possible way to make communal decisions.

First, binary voting creates winners and losers, and nobody likes to lose. As Stanford professor Harold Leavitt reminds us, "When a decision is forced quickly and when the method of deciding is by vote, what is left for the minority except psychologically to reject the decision."[23] Leavitt goes on to point out that even losers who try hard to comply with an

---

23 Leavitt, Harold J. *Management Psychology. Third Edition.* Chicago: University of Chicago Press. 1975. 216.

adverse decision are resentful about it and feel "challenged to prove that the majority decision is wrong." At best, such resentment breeds passive resistance, promotes scofflaws, and perfects the art of secret evasion. At worst, it invites open defiance–even violence and rebellion. None of this promotes good citizenship, let alone good government or economic fairness and efficiency.

To make things worse, as losers act out their resentment, the worried winners pass even more restrictive and punitive measures to reinforce their position. This spiral is one reason many laws enacted through representation, and elections for seats in guardian legislatures, are so hotly contested. Although many bills are the result of diligent compromise, and some sail through with virtual unanimity, most end up promoting one interest over another: the quid pro quo with opponents, if there is one, comes on other issues and other bills. This leaves dissenters no place to go but the streets, or back to their headquarters, coffee houses, mountain hideouts, or armories to plan obstruction, retribution, or expensive and divisive campaigns to regain legislative control. In guardian politics, we don't just get mad: we get even.

Second, since one-time binary ballots limit choices, they also limit solutions. Who says that the only choice voters should have–whether through representation or direct participation–is to accept or reject one candidate or one plan? The tacit assumption behind this method is that the item (person or proposition) on the ballot represents the best of all reasonable alternatives; that those alternatives have been examined to the satisfaction of those who must live them; and that the whole issue can be reduced to a single yes-or-no decision. If the vote is by representatives, it also assumes those guardians understand and respect the preferences of the demos and that all the talents and ideas available within that demos have been tapped to explore solutions–a nice idea, but one seldom tried, let alone mandated. (Those staples of "participatory" politics, public hearings and town-hall meetings, are often stage-managed by partisans and are aimed more at advocacy of entrenched positions than open-minded deliberation.)

While some of the talents, experience, and wisdom of the demos is reflected in the elected representative body, the candidates who fill those offices are, by virtue of their willingness to act as guardians, always undemocratic at heart. They "serve" because they want to govern others while reserving the right to govern themselves. Over the long haul, this attitude pervades the way they think and operate. At best, they become ciphers for pet ideologies, or mouthpieces for special interests and preferred groups. At worst, their actions and choices become increasingly elitist, if not aristocratic and autocratic, and reflect guardian, not citizen, values and interests. In fact as well as principle, such guardians live literally in a world of their own, governed by their own rules and their own standards of behavior.

Third, forcing majority (even super-majority) rule onto a minority or group of minorities is no substitute for building a genuine consensus within the demos. Again Leavitt reminds us that, "A good deal of research evidence shows that decisions are carried into action most effectively when they are group-consensus decisions, when all members of a group can somehow settle by their own efforts on a choice with which they all agree."[24]

Achieving consensus is not as easy as ramming through a one-time, win-lose, bare-majority victory, especially when voters in a given election are often a small fraction of the total demos. Society has been conditioned to view most conflicts as contests, and children, as well as adults, have little training, and few role models, for the consensus-making process. And consensus-building is a laborious process. It requires active listening as well as advocacy. It requires broad, creative input; give-and-take among alternatives; and acknowledgment that other viewpoints aren't necessarily evil simply because they are different. It requires institutional and individual patience. True consensus can't be forced or finessed through trickery and guile—another reason guardians and activists hate it. After all, these people want voters to endorse *their* candidate and *their* plans. They want to get on with the business of ruling and see no reason to delay or dilute their victory by accommodating different views. The last thing they want is for the demos itself to set the agenda and terms of debate, to weigh alternatives, and to construct its own solution. Even worse, from the guardian's perspective, consensus-building reduces the alienation upon which the

---

24 Ibid.

power of faction thrives. Consensus-building draws people together and reminds them that guardians, perhaps, aren't as necessary as they claim.

Perhaps the best–and best-tested–example of mandated consensus-building is found in the modern jury system. For centuries in the West, we've required consensual jury decisions for serious crimes, such as capital offenses, and it is important to understand why this venerable rule has survived so long.

In essence, consensus requires that all involved have a reasonable chance to air their views and that deliberation continue until a single opinion–a general will–emerges. In judicial trials, this almost always leads to a better interpretation of legal evidence, a discounting of lawyerly tricks, and fairer verdicts. Also, being judged by one's peers promotes better acceptance of the verdict by both litigants and the population–an important consideration when an acquitted person returns to society, or a convicted person is forcibly removed from it. Finally, a judicial system that is perceived to be fair, as well as just, will be trusted and used by more people than one that rewards skullduggery and guardian influence. This last point should not be taken lightly, because confidence in a judicial system, like any belief, is constantly tested against experience. Trust is easy to lose and hard to regain. While guardian judges may sometimes perform the jury's function, their decisions are often perceived as too legalistic, swayed too easily by technicalities or the temptations of judicial activism, and averse to common sense. We may disagree with its verdict, but even a biased jury somehow seems fairer than a biased judge.

In short, majority rule is only one way of making collective decisions–whether by guardians or by the demos itself; and if widespread acceptance and voluntary commitment to those decisions is important, it runs a poor second to consensus.

6

How Political and Economic Guardians Cooperate

THE RENAISSANCE REPRESENTED a rediscovery of classical ideals in art, technology, and trade. It also resurrected old ways of thinking about government. This reawakening of Greek and Roman ideas increased social appreciation for individuals: people who constituted the entire demos and not just the guardian elite.

Slowly, the difference between aristocrat and peasant began to shrink, at least in the eyes of the law. By the time of the Enlightenment, "natural law"–a system of rights adhering to people simply because they're human–applied even to citizens who were not significant property owners. From this perspective, fairness became something more than a deal worked out between economic and political guardians. If states could no longer command the obedience of citizens without granting them meaningful property rights, they were also obligated (in principle, at least) to extend some of the rights of property to citizens who lacked the requisite wealth. After all, people are people, and none of us choose our parents.

These new rights and freedoms–decoupled from aristocratic privilege–mobilized a substantial part of the population that had, for centuries, essentially toiled as serfs. They created new markets and new wealth, and while capitalism may not have mandated democracy, our appetite for democracy grew much stronger because of it.

The exploration of the New World and the development of the scientific method led to faster conversion of theoretical knowledge into technology and, eventually, to the Industrial Revolution. Here, production stepped out of the home and into the factory, achieving a long-sought guardian goal: centralized control over economic activity. Expanded production and trade (mainly through specialization and exchange) meant expanded markets, which led to mercantilism, the notion that a state could, and should, control the growth and distribution of its wealth. However, neither economic nor political guardians could do this alone. It demanded their active cooperation, even collaboration–and, in some cases, collusion. Under this early form of capitalism, economic guardians grew coequal with their political counterparts, especially with politicians who depended on elections to stay in power. Similarly, political guardians began to exercise more freely the economic clout that goes with sovereignty. They used their power to selectively tax, spend, and regulate behavior to forge new bonds (often in the form of rights-based legislation) directly with non-guardian citizens. These bonds, in turn, influenced the practices of private guardians.

According to Dahl, this new, integrated capitalist hierarchy depended on political guardians' ability to employ state-sanctioned violence to protect (or leave unprotected, if that was their choice) the property of economic guardians as well as to enforce their own political will.[25] This helped private-sector guardians extract surplus from the economy while giving preferred groups of citizens easy access to capital and special regulatory protection. It also made sure the educational process served guardian needs by producing compliant citizen-workers and voters who did not rock boat.

Unfortunately this accommodation, while great for mass production, resulted also in mass alienation–of craftspeople from their craft, of producers from their customers, of citizens from the land that claimed them– causing a nosedive in personal pride and a reduced sense of community in a substantial part of the population. Because political guardians, especially in the nineteenth century, so often sided with economic guardians at the expense of citizen-workers, state power came to be seen more and more as a resource available mostly to the monied class, a perception that persists– and not without cause–to this day.

Theorists like Rousseau, Mill, and Hobbes concluded that, in one way or another, government's basic job was defining the "common good"

---

25 Dahl. *Democracy and Its Critics.*

and achieving the "general will" of the demos. Until the late eighteenth century, these terms had been used by public and private guardians as code words for their own interests. What was good for all citizens, including non-guardians, and what society as a whole might want, seldom registered and was thought by many to be irrelevant or unknowable. If it was mentioned at all, it was as rhetorical window-dressing to make guardian preferences more palatable to the public. This pattern changed little in the nineteenth and twentieth centuries, although populism, including plebiscitary politics, was becoming a stronger force. For most of this period, though, politics was a zero-sum game played by, and for, guardians and their preferred groups. Monopoly over legislation and the coercive power of the state was prized not only because of its ability to advance guardian causes, but also for its potential to protect winners from retribution by the losers.

From the mid-nineteenth century to the turn of the twentieth century, American economic guardians protected their property rights and social/political prerogatives mostly through private means: by pooling investments, forming trusts, and creating vertical monopolies. The New Deal, commonly assumed to be the U.S. government's reaction to capitalist failures that caused the Great Depression was, more accurately, a long deferred and very public display of the power state guardians always held in the industrial age but were reluctant to use. In this sense, Roosevelt's New Dealers were less "meddlesome socialists" intruding into private enterprise than silent partners who had suddenly become very vocal about how the nation's political economy was being managed. The Great Depression was a great embarrassment—and liability—to the integrated guardian hierarchy, not just its private component. State guardians therefore demanded, and got, a bigger piece of the pie, to be paid in coin most meaningful to politicians: more taxes and more power to deliver benefits to preferred groups. One of these concessions was the unprecedented buildup of government bureaucracy—a "standing army" of administrators and regulators who could implement state guardians' will and insulate elected officials, to some degree, from the negative consequences of their own acts.

This is the true source and nature of the so-called rift between big government and big business. They are like two playground bullies squabbling over a ball, united mainly in their determination to keep anyone else from playing the game. Neither wants the average citizen to participate in their day-to-day agenda-setting and decision-making; but their periodic disagreements require them, occasionally and separately, to appeal to the general public. In this sense, the non-guardian demos—"the people" we so often hear about—are less the source of all state power than an occasional tie-breaker in sibling rivalries; a sleeping dog all guardians would just as soon let lie.

In the years following World War II, the burdens of political guardianship (an expensive bureaucracy plus the plethora of expanding programs needed to win new friends and satisfy old allies) grew faster than the benefits public guardians could deliver. In the world of representative democracy, however, this social and financial "red ink" did not lead to bankruptcy and reform, but to more promises, greater spending, and inflation—not to mention institutionalized waste. Budget overruns begat bigger budgets, and cumbersome, ineffectual policies only spawned more red tape. Citizens on the lowest socioeconomic rungs became a permanent underclass and their potential for social disruption became a persuasive argument for increased guardian power. Private guardians, too, became addicted to the perks that went with their accommodation. These included not just tax breaks and beneficial regulations for favored industries, but more laws aimed at perpetuating non-democratic corporate governance.

Seeing how this system worked, non-guardian citizen-workers began organizing into groups that emphasized identity and special-interests: a host of squeaky wheels all clamoring for grease. By the 1980s, this "system" had devolved into nothing less than a low-intensity civil war, or social war, whose weapons were group identity, single-issue politics, individual anomie and alienation, civil disobedience (and occasional public disorder), judicial crusades, legal harassment, and the death of even the pretense that representative guardianship was somehow concerned with the common good and general will.

One result of all this was a tendency to define fairness not as the product of consensual processes and adherence to mutually agreed-upon principles, but as the victory of one aggrieved group over another. Self-perpetuating bureaucracies and guardians in both the public and private sectors came to owe allegiance not to their constituents, but to the integrated hierarchy that kept them in power—characteristics of a true "ruling class."[26] Liberal capitalist representative democracy found its biggest threat came not from fascism, communism, or socialism—all of which featured their own brand of guardianism and were, at one time or another, openly allied with U.S. interests—but from ordinary people who sought to substitute popular power for guardian rule, to make exclusionary governance more inclusive.

The primary mission of guardianism, therefore, became not just the arbitration of one set of interests versus another—a myth designed to keep dependents infatuated with guardians and see them as indispensable—but the preservation of guardian control over the entire political economy, keeping non-guardians out of the loop. Isaiah Berlin articulated the creed of these "armed prophets" thus: "I know which way to drive the human caravan; and since you are ignorant of what I know, you cannot be allowed to have liberty of choice even within the narrowest limits... I know what you need, what all men need; and if there is resistance...it must be broken and hundreds of thousands may have to perish to make millions happy for all time."[27]

This is not, and never was, the voice of the people; it is the roar of a leviathan—and its blast withers the buds of both civitas and societas.

In a corporation, for example, the board of directors' ostensible duty is to look after the interests of shareholders, the nominal owners. Similarly, in a representative democracy, elected officials—the political equivalent of the corporate board—are supposed to look after the interests of the demos. The corporation's employees are analogous to the government's bureaucracy; they are the people who actually get things done. Ownership and

---

26 Two typical examples were reported on the same date in California in 2001. In the first case, Governor Gray Davis demoted a state lawyer "whose interpretation of labor laws angered employer groups from retailers to Silicon Valley..." (Lucas, Greg. "Davis demotes labor lawyer for state," *San Francisco Chronicle*, June 28, 2001). In the second, an out-of-state developer was told by a San Francisco bureaucrat to hire a prominent state senator, a friend and ally of the city's mayor, as a "consultant" if he expected to participate in a lucrative waterfront deal. (Finnie, Chuck; Strasburg, Jenny; and Williams, Lance. "N.Y. developer says Burton was touted for lobbyist job: SF port director allegedly urged hiring," *San Francisco Chronicle*, June 28, 2001.)

27 Berlin, Isaiah. "On the Pursuit of the Ideal," *New York Review of Books*, March 17, 1988.

sovereignty are distinct in both cases and theoretically rest with a specific constituency, although directors and executives (in the private sector) and politicians and appointed officials (in the public), who exercise day-to-day control over workers and bureaucrats, often view constituent interest very differently from the way those owners and sovereigns might view it themselves.

In the eyes of political guardians, the public's main function is to "purchase" with their votes and taxes the "products and services" the government provides. Just as corporate boards of directors and executives want to please shareholders by operating at a profit, top bureaucrats want to make their elected and appointed political patrons look good by maximizing praise, and minimizing complaints, from the groups upon which those guardians depend for their position. Pleasing the upper strata of the integrated guardian hierarchy is the way lower- and mid-level guardians keep their jobs and get promoted. In government, backing up political promises with bureaucratic action keeps incumbents safe, keeps campaign contributions flowing, and prevents public policy from changing too often, which causes administrative and legal headaches for those who must implement that policy directly.

This, at any rate, is how the system has come to work. Guardians in both the private and public spheres face remarkably similar relationships, structures, motivations, and mechanisms; they are really two subsystems of same political economy—two sides of the same power-wielding coin, joined like Siamese twins by the umbilicus that nourishes them both: the taxpayer-consumer's wallet. In reality, neither politicians and top bureaucrats nor corporate directors and executives are especially beholding to their respective constituents. They are bound instead to the upper-tier guardians who hire them and whose patronage results in bigger budgets, better perks, and more power.

Although each has its favorite methods for preserving and increasing power, political guardians have historically been a bit more savvy than economic guardians about treading the narrow line between oligarchy and democracy—of giving citizen-dependents a sense that they are still at the center of the political process instead of its periphery. This is partly because political guardians depend regularly on popular votes and public opinion polls to get their way; whereas corporate guardians, depending mostly on other guardians and the courts, find it easier to exclude whomever they choose.

Nonetheless, citizens' gradual awareness of their political rights has led them to demand more say in economic matters as well. "More say" in this case means not just consultation (giving advice that guardians may freely ignore), but participating in the major, binding decisions that govern a firm. To the degree that this participation is representative (as when corporate guardians add outside stakeholders to the board of directors), it is an extension of guardianism; which is one reason why corporations accept these accommodations so readily–they change very little. To the extent that stakeholders participate directly and in large numbers, as in the occasional, meaningful proxy fight, such reforms can be truly democratic; though both private- and public-sector guardians strive mightily to see that these occasions are few and far between.

This raises the question of that unique brand of conflict resolution called competition, the free and unfettered use of which is often called the essence of free enterprise. If this were true, you would think that economic and political guardians would do more to promote it. At minimum, it would mean streamlining transactions and facilitating the flow of information, giving buyers more complete and objective facts about prices, costs, and the difference between them–profits. You would also think these disclosures would be regulated at least as well as the information given by firms to investors, and that products would be proven safe and effective, that job conditions would be safe and sanitary, and that workers' compensation would be fair–for all these factors contribute to a firm's competitive posture in both input (labor and raw materials) and output (goods and services) markets.

But which "government" is ultimately accountable for ensuring that this fabled competition actually occurs? Elected representatives? The executive branch? Bureaucrats? Judges? Or the demos who is supposed to be sovereign over all? And on the private side, which part of the corporation is ultimately responsible for observing society's rules about competitive fair play and paying the penalty for noncompliance? Top executives and directors? Managers and workers? Or the shareholders who are supposedly the company's sovereign?

We can see now the corner into which our current system has painted itself. Market regulations, as well as the penalties for violating them, are handled like virtually everything else in our political economy: by a non-democratic accommodation between public and private guardians. These guardians are like adults arguing an umpire's call at a little-league game: some are coaches with a track record to protect and some are simply parents with dependents they want to help–but their arguments ultimately have less to do with sports and more to do with status and comparative advantage. As Heilbroner puts it: "The economic domain is simply of one piece with the political... capitalism represents 'the ultimate privatization of politics'... ."[28] This doesn't mean that private and public guardians at all times consciously conspire to place special interests, including their own, above the common good and general will; only that, by the very nature of guardianism, that's what usually happens.

To illustrate, let's look more closely at how corporate boards of directors cultivate allies among elected officials, since both must periodically turn to some kind of demos (shareholders in the first case, citizen-taxpayers in the second) to stay in power.

Politicians need just enough clout–the "clubs are trumps" power of sovereignty–over private guardians to preserve their place in the integrated hierarchy. This means they must occasionally placate non-guardian citizens, the bulk of the population, who are otherwise prevented from meaningful participation in making binding decisions about their jobs and communities. For their part, corporate directors often serve on multiple boards, increasing their clout within and between industries, and therefore increasing their bargaining power when it comes to making deals with public guardians. If you doubt this happens to any significant degree, read any publicly held company's notice for the annual meeting in which directors are "elected" and executive compensation is set. New directors are not elected from a slate of candidates arising from the company's "demos" (its broad base of shareholders), but are nominated—noncompetitively–by current board members whose selections are then ratified (usually, rubber-stamped) in a shareholder vote. If you peruse the resumes of these candidates, you'll find that their common denominator is not resemblance to the average shareholder, but prior membership in the corporate guardians' club. Virtually all are, or have been, key executives in complementary or competing industries and sit on multiple boards–elite members of an

---

28 Heilbroner. *Nature and Logic*. 86, 100.

already very exclusive circle. When it comes to top executives' salaries, sharp increases in compensation are invariably justified by the claim that they are "comparable to other firms in the industry." Similarly, public officials justify big raises for top bureaucrats by saying such increases are needed "to keep talented administrators from joining the private sector." The intent of such salary-fixing may or may not be collusive, but the result certainly is. Top guardians make top dollar because guardians, not their constituents, make these key decisions.

This de facto collusion goes far beyond cultural kinship and personal greed, which are probably its most trivial aspects. Corporate executives and government bureaucrats often share the same policy interests, since top leaders in both sectors usually spring from the same educational institutions and follow similar career paths, often rotating between high-level corporate and government positions. Both must live with the decisions of the other, so it makes sense to cooperate, if not collaborate, even when those decisions are ostensibly independent. After a while, it's only natural for these guardians to begin looking at their spheres of influence as a private preserve, and the quid pro quos exchanged among them as essential for "doing business" in that area.

Worst of all, even if their sense of stewardship for non-guardians is strong, their authority is still autocratic and oligarchic, not democratic. We are at the mercy of their moods and calculations, of their prejudices and whims. Conflicting views are heard only at their sufferance, and then after clearing appropriate gatekeepers. If it's lonely at the top, it's because our guardian hierarchy has made it so.

The mechanisms by which these collegial guardians achieve their ends are tangible favors: seeking or dispensing tax relief and other favorable regulations; awarding or receiving government contracts; and granting or seeking taxpayer subsidies. Political guardians can also punish private guardians by selectively increasing taxes and regulatory burdens, or by focusing public scrutiny on those who don't play the game. Political guardians also have the power to transfer private diseconomies—such as the cost of cleaning up factory pollution, or bailing out troubled industries—to the public sector, while requiring other, less-favored industries to shoulder such costs themselves. They can also use the bully pulpit of high office—politicians' ready access to the media and high-profile legislative hearings—to fine-tune citizen perceptions.

The intensity and overtness of this symbiosis shifts with economic and political currents. In good times, citizen-watchdogs either tend to look the other way or find few ears for their complaints. Since World War II, the advance of Keynesianism (government management of aggregate demand, with private profits being the main criterion for allocating resources) and the growth of the welfare state (firms and individuals rebating of a portion of their income to the government so it can mitigate social problems and placate dissent) went hand-in-hand. This accommodation did nothing to correct the shortcomings inherent in the system; in fact, it perpetuated them by transferring responsibility for diseconomies away from the private sector and toward public guardians, who are held accountable by different standards.

Periodic grass-roots agitation for true democratic reform serves mostly to strengthen the bonds between private and public guardians, since a group under attack tends to close ranks and band together. In periods of actual or potential guardian crisis, such as the Clinton impeachment and the Bush-Gore electoral stalemate, some public guardians actually found it necessary to remind Americans that they live not in a democracy, but in a republic, where there are some matters that the "sovereign people" just don't have any business meddling with.

In short, free enterprise has come to mean neither the freedom of corporations from government interference nor the freedom of government to interfere with them, but the freedom of both types of guardians from interference by non-guardian stakeholders. Globalization of what had previously been national economies–and the traumatic, rolling financial crises that seem a permanent part of that landscape–showed Keynesianism to be what monetarists always said it was, a poor substitute for following a few general rules about growing the money supply and underscored once again the wisdom of broad-based, decentralized decision-making.

As it turns out, there are real limits to guardians' ability to control aggregate demand. The high cost of the resulting entitlement economy–from unaffordable health care to bankrupt public utilities and a culture of self-serving corporate executives–eventually overwhelms its productive elements, making political guardians look foolish and inept, and its economic guardians look greedy and short-sighted.

There had to be a better way, and a key piece to that puzzle was *profits*.

7

Guardians and Private Profit

CLASSICAL ECONOMICS DEFENDS profit on a variety of grounds: some logical, some intuitive. Most arguments, however, are based on wishful thinking about how people should behave in a world of imperfect markets and passive worker-consumers.

Traditionally, profit implies economy. You can't have a surplus of anything, including money, until what comes in exceeds what goes out. This is a polite way of saying that profit only occurs when the buyer pays "too much" for a service or commodity: the price exceeds the sum of all costs that went into providing it, including the cost of capital. If profit is "normal"–that is, if it is not so high that it drives buyers away but is still high enough to keep producers in that business–the economy "gets by" in that particular market. It lurches from one state of equilibrium to another, as prices asked and quantities demanded fluctuate–depending on changing tastes, the cost and availability of labor and raw materials, contributions from new technology, the number of new firms entering the market, and so on. What doesn't change (or changes by only a small amount) is the seller's markup: typically, a modest percentage of total cost. This markup, or profit, allows the company to reward certain stakeholders whose compensation is not a usual or necessary element of total cost, such as dividends to shareholders.

Unfortunately, mature markets tend eventually toward oligopoly or monopoly. In these real-world markets, "normal" profit is too low because it forces firms to concentrate on minimizing costs, which is hard to do when workers demand higher wages, managers want bigger salaries and bonuses, suppliers increase their prices, taxes and regulatory expenses rise, and investors and lenders seek higher returns. It's much easier–and more rewarding to all concerned–for private guardians to create market conditions that support higher-than-normal profits.

One way to do this is to minimize competition with the help of regulatory guardians, who can raise legal barriers to market entry, creating an environment that favors established firms. Another is with the cooperation of financial guardians, such as institutional investors and big lenders, who can grant favorable terms to established firms (the larger, the better) and make the economic cost of entry so high that it discourages new competitors. While steps like these may enhance the firm's bottom-line, they tend to drive up prices and limit consumer choices–not what free markets are supposed to be about.

Even worse, greater-than-normal profits take money out of the hands of buyers, who may have better uses for it (including savings, investment, or spending in other areas) and concentrates it in the hands of guardians who, insulated from competitive forces, have fewer incentives to manage it wisely. Even sellers in this supposedly advantageous position eventually find their options limited, since they are hesitant to risk their current, predictable high return by investing in new products–another traditional use for profits. As resources continue to be misallocated to these less-competitive, bloated firms, new products and new markets fail to materialize, and the whole economy gradually becomes worse off. In short, what begins as a dream come true for one firm or industry becomes a nightmare for everybody. If the common good, in this case, is more, better, and less expensive products for more people, it is unlikely that the production, pricing, and political decisions that led to an oligopolized or monopolized market would have been made by the community at large.

A second argument for private profit is that economic surplus is the engine that drives social progress. After all, society is better off when unprofitable firms fail, reallocating resources to firms that will use them more efficiently and please more customers. And public sector guardians can always use the extra income provided by taxes, which usually depend on profit. While the first part may be true in the early stages of market development, mature markets tend to stifle, not promote, competition. Profits rise not because of increased demand, better products, or more efficient use of resources, but because pricing has become inelastic. In other words, prices go up simply because they *can* go up without penalizing sales—at least to a point beyond which they would trigger consumer revolt and regulatory backlash. Money to pay for this extra profit must come from somewhere, and it is siphoned away from other uses to which the community might have put it. Again, it's hard to imagine that the firm's broadest base of stakeholders—its lenders, investors, employees, customers, suppliers, regulators, community neighbors, and so on, acting together on a consensual basis—would make the same pricing and production decisions as a handful of well-insulated corporate guardians.

Of course, this still begs the question of whether less-profitable firms deserve to fail simply because other firms, for whatever reason (including collusion with politicians and exploitation of employees and customers), manage to create a bigger surplus. Should the same rule apply to individuals, households, and families? After all, the provident often suffer along with the impecunious when a big employer downsizes or goes bankrupt. Should these bystanders (really, stakeholders) be punished because a particular firm chose not to charge its customers "too much"? Even more to the point, why should one form of inefficiency—inelastic pricing, for example—be permitted (or even facilitated by political guardians) while other kinds of inefficiency are punished, especially when the social cost of the preferred inefficiency is borne by society as a whole while its benefits are enjoyed by a few? Again, these questions are less economic than moral and social; but they're all related to the high price we ultimately pay for guardianism.

A third rationale for private (and especially for higher-than-normal) profit is that return is, or should be, proportional to risk. An entrepreneur or property owner should be rewarded for inventing new technology, constructing new facilities, and gambling on satisfying consumer wants. Sources of capital—big lenders and institutional investors, including venture capitalists—use the same argument: that the "bets" they lose on many unsuccessful ventures must be compensated for by higher-than-normal returns on the relative handful that succeed.

On closer inspection, though, neither of these rationales holds water. Entrepreneurs do indeed take a risk when they start a new enterprise, but so do their employees, their suppliers (at least those who extend them credit), their customers (who depend on product safety and quality, availability of parts, warrantees, and customer service), and so on. Few of these people participate in the strategic decisions that guide the firm or share the super-normal profits that may result. Nonetheless they certainly are asked to share in losses should the firm become insolvent and seek court protection from its creditors–as has become a standard contingency in many modern business plans, with no stigma or shame attached.[29]

As to the justification of extra-normal profit for the providers of capital: the dirty little secret here is that financial backers don't reward risk at all, they reward market advantage, which (although some risk may be associated with it initially) is something completely different, and which can be achieved in a variety of ways that have nothing to do with thrift, improving the land, or inventing a better mousetrap. For example, realizing a profit from investment in a firm that promises to make a faster computer chip involves three main contingencies: (a) that the company will actually deliver the chip; (b) that the chip will be superior to, and more price competitive than its competitors; and (c) that computer makers will demand it in sufficient quantities to make production profitable. These outcomes are uncertain, it's true, but the probability of any particular one occurring–and therefore the particular level of profit or loss that will go with it–can be analyzed, and investors can hedge their "bet" appropriately. What's truly risky is trying to satisfy needs for which market probabilities are unknown–like providing health care to the poor or fielding a practical alternative to the internal combustion engine. Because the market performance of these risky ventures is unclear, capitalists generally avoid funding them, regardless of the potential social or economic benefit–factors that might be more important to a broader base of stakeholders making similar allocation decisions.

Finally, it is not the occasional, successful entrepreneur who rewards financiers and makes them whole from previous "bad bets," it is the

---

29 One egregious example of this was the highly publicized bankruptcy of Pacific Gas & Electric Corporation, which gave its top executives huge raises just hours before its bankruptcy filing in 2001, triggered by the firm's biggest loss in a hundred years. Not surprisingly, company officials defended their actions by saying such raises were "comparable to those given to executives running similar businesses." (Lazarus, David. "PG&E Posts Worst Loss In Firm's History," *San Francisco Chronicle*, April 17, 2001.)

community–principally the firm's customers–who pay that excess profit. Entrepreneurs are important players, to be sure, but they are not the only ones. Their privileged status–the ability to allocate resources arbitrarily and profit disproportionately from a venture's success–comes mainly from traditional guardian rights in property, and not from anything inherent in the production process.

Again, these are primarily moral and social questions whose economic component, while important, has been given inordinate weight in a value system set up primarily to serve the interests of guardians, not their stakeholders. There is no reason to think that a more broadly based, consensual method of allocating capital to new ventures and determining (and distributing) the profit therefrom would be notably less efficient than the guardian-based system, and there are many reasons to suppose it would be a great deal fairer.

A fourth argument for extra-normal profit is that hefty surpluses permit the formation of extra capital, both human and material. That is, the more money economic guardians make (as profit, not just a return of principal) the more money they can return to the community in the form of new lending and investment, corporate charity, and improved worker benefits. While corporate altruism is not unknown and modern companies are much more aware of their social responsibilities today than in the past, there is no compelling reason why such surpluses–if buyers are otherwise willing to provide them–should be filtered first through guardian coffers. Why should corporate executives decide how that portion of market surplus earmarked as "social profit" be spent?–especially since those guardians will be tempted to use some or all of it as contributions to political guardians, as dividends to shareholders, or simply to award higher salaries, bonuses, or stock options to themselves.[30] Referring to the Enron scandal

---

30 The sudden bankruptcy of Enron Corporation in December 2001 provides an egregious example of self-serving executives. These guardians made heavy donations to their political counterparts while enriching themselves at the expense of shareholders and employees–many of which lost their retirement savings–when excessive profits from the year's energy crisis, inflated through creative accounting, allowed guardians controlling Enron's pension fund to prevent employees from cashing out, as the executives did, before a national scandal erupted. (Coile, Zachary and Berthelsen, Christian. "Criminal investigation of Enron: Justice Dept. wants to know if energy giant fleeced investors, workers,"

of 2001, in which top executives used their guardian positions and inside information to profit from inflated stock values while many shareholders and employees lost their life saving, the Washington Post's E.J. Dionne Jr. notes, "For a very long time, we've assumed that the fundamental conflict in capitalism is between owners and the workers. Enron proves that the real conflict is between insiders and outsiders. The losers in the Enron case are both stockholders and workers. This suggests a new form of politics both inside corporations and in the country as a whole."[31]

The point is that while consensual decisions about the way surplus is used may result in the same distribution, a broader base of stakeholders would likely have wiser and fairer ideas about what to do with it.

Finally, guardians argue that big profits allow firms to grow faster than the growth permitted by normal profit. When it flows liberally, it nourishes all the firm's stakeholders, from new hires and suppliers to consumers who enjoy new products as well as the government that depends on corporate and employee incomes for taxes. What guardians don't mention is that surplus usually runs much deeper in real corporations than the number that shows up on the bottom line. In addition to huge salaries and other executive perks—from company cars and company condos to housing subsidies for CEO mansions—top executives regularly take large bonuses and stock options, *all* of which are accounted as corporate expenses, not as profit participation. And these are only a few of the ways the law treats these corporate queen bees differently from the drones who make the honey. Unlike individuals, who must borrow or save before they can invest, the fictitious corporate "person" can issue new equity—essentially, make the pie bigger by widening it with a rolling pin—an option just not available to real, flesh-and-blood people.

Further, guardians controlling corporate assets often create surpluses by cutting costs that do not affect them personally, sometimes increasing their own compensation as a reward for clever "fat trimming." In a

---

San Francisco Chronicle, January 10, 2002; and Yardley, Jim, Barboza, David, and Van Natta, Don. "Lay's political savvy backfires: Insider status now under scrutiny," New York Times (San Francisco Chronicle), February 3, 2002.)

31 Dionne, E.J. Jr. "New class politics is good for capitalism," San Francisco Chronicle, February 22, 2002.

1997 study of executive compensation in recently downsized firms, two nonpartisan research groups discovered that "layoff leaders" experienced an average increase in total compensation that was 13 percent higher than executives of firms that found other ways to reduce expenses, cut losses, or increase their profits.[32] This percentage rose even higher in the year 2000, when a deepening recession caused even more big firms to "cut fat" by cutting employment. According to a *Business Week* survey, CEOs of the 52 major companies laying off at least 1,000 workers paid themselves on average a whopping 80 percent more than CEOs of big corporations who dealt with the downturn in other, more humane ways.[33]

Even when employment is not affected, well-insulated corporate guardians can use their position to prosper in the worst of times. According to U.C. Berkeley professor (and former management compensation consultant) Graef Crystal, between the mid-1970s and mid-1990s, compensation for a typical American CEO rose from 35 times to 120 times the pay of the average manufacturing worker–and this differential only increased when the comparison was extended to other industries.[34] On average, a CEO in the United States can count on making 160 times what his average employee earns. Even worse, in a similar study conducted by Crystal for the United Shareholders Association, in which objective criteria were applied to normalize pay differences due to company size and performance, 521 of the 920 executives surveyed (over 56 percent) were found to be overpaid. While company size accounted for about 30 percent of this variation, performance accounted for no more than 4 percent, leaving, in Crystal's words, "about 66 percent of the differences in CEO pay not explainable by the two things that ought to explain virtually all of the differences."[35]

---

32 McLeod, Ramon G., "CEOs Being Rewarded for Dropping the Ax," *San Francisco Chronicle*, May 1, 1997.

33 Gordon, Marcy. Associated Press. "Job-cutting CEOs had highest pay: Layoff leaders earned 80% more, study finds," *San Francisco Chronicle*, September 2, 2001.

34 *San Jose Mercury News*, "Consultant Targets CEO Salaries," *Marin Independent Journal*, December 30, 1991.

35 Gruley, Bryan Gannet News Service. "Executive Pay and Performance: It Doesn't Add Up," *Marin Independent Journal*, November 16, 1991.

What does explain this discrepancy? One obvious reason is the tendency of any well-entrenched power hierarchy to serve itself first. Guardians of any kind quickly form their own society which is separate and above the demos that anoints and tolerates them. This by itself may not make profit undemocratic, but it certainly suggests that stakeholders rather than guardians would make better custodians of so potent a resource.

The advent of an integrated guardian hierarchy created another big barrier to the further merging of individual rights with property rights, and to the development of fairer, more consensual methods for allocating resources, including profits.

As capitalism matured and became more institutionalized, political choice began to resemble consumer choice, and political activity took on the color of market action. Citizen-workers weren't expected to exert direct influence on their government. They were expected merely to "shop with their ballots" among competing candidates, who marketed themselves aggressively both to voters and to the economic guardians who became their biggest campaign contributors.

This development did nothing to increase citizen control over, or the accountability of, political guardians; but it went a long way toward commodifying the electoral process—turning campaigns into exercises in image-making, candidate-packaging, and advertising. The legislative process, too, became a marketplace where lobbyists and interest/identity groups invested in the careers of individual politicians in expectation of a promised return. It also cast the cold shadow of covert governance over the entire political economy. It assumed that political guardians were somehow as entitled to privacy in making their deals as economic guardians were in making theirs.

Gradually, this linkage became the rationale for holding government officials responsible for the overall economic health of the nation. Political guardians asked voters to evaluate their performance based on their ability to coerce or cajole big business into generating an adequate surplus. These public guardians, who had largely replaced family and church as the principal arbiters of moral standards, were now seen as the agents of prosperity as well. Grass-roots democratic input was confined mostly to special-interest lobbying and the usual tactics of the marginalized and voiceless: demonstrations, protests, strikes, and boycotts. Political micro-management, such as wage and price controls in certain industries and policing the working conditions in others, meant that big questions such as deciding just who should participate in making these decisions were ignored. As a result, guardians and their preferred groups became better off while out-of-favor groups gradually became worse off. The seamless fusion of state power with the power of property came to be seen not as an exception to long-term historical trends (such as those that produced the joint-stock company and citizen initiatives and referenda), but as the rule that made them happen.

In reality, capitalism (which always bore the faint stain of elitism) and free enterprise (which has strong, if unjustified, democratic connotations) are really two different things. Firms like competition only when they are trying to enter a new market; after that, they prefer oligopoly or monopoly–a decidedly non-competitive and unfree market situation. Investors, after all, are not motivated by risk, but the expectation of gain. Lenders, in particular, worship at the shrine of low-risk returns, using their power to ration capital to keep its "price"–interest rates and a growing variety of fees–a bit higher than necessary.

In all of this, political guardians act mainly to protect the interests of existing holders of capital, as in the infamous 1998 government-orchestrated bailout of trendy but over-extended Long-Term Capital Management by a consortium of financiers who had personal, as well as institutional, interests in the company.[36] When the government finally does intervene in a monopolized market–almost always at the last possible moment and after considerable public outcry–it does not act to restore a low-friction, competitive market (a condition of more perfect competition); it relieves the current owners of property and the current suppliers of capital from any serious risk of true loss, especially the loss of their ability to command future surpluses. Typically, showcase price or operating controls are temporarily imposed, followed by the application of anti-trust litigation that is so protracted that it invariably allows the offending

---

36 Fraser, Andrew. Associated Press. "Firms Act as Investor, Lender: Critics say hedge fund bailout smacks of conflict of interest," *San Francisco Chronicle*, October 7, 1998.

private guardians to quietly reallocate their holdings, over time, from one area of economic concentration to another–and the cycle begins again.

If you doubt that this happens in real life, compare the breakup of AT&T in the 1980s with the post-divestiture telecommunications market ten or fifteen years later. A few big companies still provide most of the same services, and a few have added related new services, like cable television, which only increases their market power–and even the so-called Baby Bells have started to recombine. Similarly, airline deregulation of that same era did not create better, cheaper airline service for all, but resulted in a few highly competitive routes embedded within a structure of more expensive and restrictive service to everywhere else–not to mention fewer airlines and skies filled with aircraft that are demonstrably less safe, plus Draconian cuts to passenger amenities.[37] In testimony to a Senate oversight committee, a Department of Transportation official confessed that after 20-years of airline deregulation, consumers generally faced higher fares and fewer choices in most areas. He attributed this to the way large airlines dominate key hub cities and hamper new carriers (aided and abetted by airport authorities) through takeoff and landing time restrictions, excessive gate leasing fees, and limiting access to certain cities from hub airports. Where price competition exists, it is used to drive smaller carriers out of business, after which fares are restored to higher levels. Look also at California's very expensive experiment with public utility "deregulation." Instead of unleashing market power to bring more and cheaper energy to an expanding population, it actually caused blackouts and astronomical price increases to those consumers and businesses not included on the guardian hierarchy's list of favored companies, such as Southern California Edison, which was bailed out at taxpayers' expense, and Pacific Gas & Electric, which consigned those assets not previously transferred to its parent holding company to the protection of bankruptcy court.[38] This very avoidable crisis was caused when a consortium of energy-gobbling private guardians–steel, mining, and cement producers, as well as numerous high-

---

37 Dobbyn, Tim. (Reuters). "Airline Competition Has Declined, Panel Told." *San Francisco Chronicle*. March 6, 1998.

38 Berthelsen, Christian. "Genesis of State's Energy Fiasco," *San Francisco Chronicle*, December 11, 2000.

tech companies, to name only a few—wanted access to the cheaper electricity available from independent producers. Using their clout with the state legislature, they forced big utilities to go out of the power production business and buy power at the independents' prices. Inevitably, those independent producers (the notorious Enron Corporation included) used their new market power to withhold supplies and bid prices up to obscene new levels, which eventually affected ordinary citizens. Since public guardians could not let the lights go out in California, they used taxpayer money to pick up the tab—to subsidize wholesale energy purchases and, in some cases, go into the utilities business themselves.

The same sad pattern appeared in the deregulation of cable television and banks. A 2002 Consumers Union study concluded that deregulation had resulted in decreased services and increased prices in both industries. In banking, predatory lending and hidden fees drove up consumer costs well above those experienced in the regulated 1980s. In cable television, increases in monthly fees have continually exceeded the rate of inflation and viewer satisfaction, says James Guest, the organization's president, is "bottom of the barrel."[39]

---

39 Geewax, Marilyn. Cox News. "Deregulation not working, Consumers Union says" *San Francisco Chronicle*, June 11, 2002.

8
Guardianism and the Law

THROUGHOUT HISTORY, most laws were passed piecemeal to deal with specific problems as they arose, often in emergencies. Until what we might call the constitutional era–from the Magna Carta onward–there was no general framework against which new laws could be judged. "Legal memory," an informal consensus among guardians about why old laws had been passed and why some worked and others didn't, guided lawmakers, lawgivers, magistrates, and juries in interpreting and enforcing certain statutes. Interpretations or new laws that drifted too far from this consensus provoked guardian or citizen resistance. Our ancestors may not have been legal experts, but they knew which laws they liked.

One idea central to constitutions is that any law, no matter how powerful its maker, is subject to review against some higher, transcending authority. Unfortunately, to guarantee their monopoly on coercive power, sovereign guardians such as kings–Hobbes' leviathan incarnate— often had to exempt themselves from the laws they made for others. They became, in essence, citizens with unlimited rights; vessels into which citizen-dependents deposited their natural rights so that their guardian-protectors could exercise those rights on their behalf.[40]

The leviathan concept satisfied most people most of the time, but certain nobles (who often had more wealth and power than the king they

---

40 Johnston, David. *The Rhetoric of Leviathan: Thomas Hobbes and the Politics of Cultural Transformation*. Princeton: Princeton University Press. 1986.

served), sometimes chafed under a sovereign's arbitrary laws. Gradually, these nobles demanded not only more rights, but that the king himself should behave as if those laws, particularly the ones protecting individual rights in property, bound the monarchy as well. This was the essence of the Magna Carta: the "great charter" that became, more or less, the basis for the constitutions of virtually all English-speaking countries.

As English society evolved and significant property took forms other than landed estates, rights originally applied to property were applied in other areas. Liberties became attached to individuals, not just to positions and hereditary titles–a crucial step toward true democracy as well as republicanism. By the sixteenth century, the "unwritten" part of Britain's constitution had become a significant part of its law. Political rights meant not just access by ordinary people to the processes by which collective decisions were made (mostly through the election of parliamentary representatives), but access to state protection when the owners of property went too far in exploiting tenants and workers.

The real significance of this evolution had less to do with grass-roots democratic empowerment than the linking of personal liberty, property, and political choice into a seamless whole. In the constitutional age, individual rights–civil and legal–became alternate ways for creating, allocating, and distributing wealth, as well as making political choices. Just as important, the forced sharing of rights previously held exclusively by those at the top of the guardian pyramid tended to undermine the principle of guardianism itself. This weakening of what had previously been a rather monolithic power structure–guardians over dependents–gave rise not only to more democratic institutions, but an appetite for democracy that has steadily increased.

Of course, democratic leveling did not eliminate all social, economic, and political injustice, nor did it seriously threaten guardianism. Possessing a right did not guarantee one's ability to use it. In many cases, oppressive capitalist relationships merely replaced oppressive feudal relationships. But increased freedom of opportunity did increase the amount of participation and consent available at any given level in society. Depending on the international and economic situation, individual rights might be emphasized in one era, while collective rights might be emphasized in another. Thus, democratic participation in a rights-oriented society seldom experiences equilibrium for long; rather it oscillates continually, like prices in a stock market, losing ground one day but making up for it the next, compounding its returns over many years. In the very long run, if the underlying constitution is strong, the general level of meaningful participation rises steadily, its swings amplified or dampened by the actions of its guardians.

This raises the all-important question of "legal positivism" versus "legal realism": how much power should judicial guardians have in unilaterally interpreting a constitution that is meant to apply to everyone?

At the time the U.S. Constitution was framed, guardians thought the law was, and ought to be, objective and politically neutral—an idea called legal positivism. That is, the law could and should be understood in its own terms, according to timeless legal principles in the same way scientists understand nature by discovering and applying natural laws. A century and a half after the U.S. Constitution was ratified, however, both a great civil war and a devastating economic depression had changed this view considerably. Public guardians in a powerful central government now imagined its social contract was not with the demos as a whole, but with specific groups of citizen-dependents, as well as traditional economic guardians. Legal realism, as this idea was known, had by the end of the 1930s largely replaced a belief in legal positivism in the minds of liberal theorists. While continuing to dress the law in trappings of objectivity, proponents of legal realism knew that most real-world judges exercised great power in deciding which legal precedents and principles would apply in important cases. These judges also determined how those principles and precedents were interpreted, drawing ideas from such extra-legal disciplines as psychology, sociology, and political science. Just as important, their decisions determined how law and legal theory would be taught in law schools, influencing future generations of public and private guardians.

This new view of constitutions and legality, also called sociological jurisprudence, held that laws are created mostly as a result of struggles between competing interests. For example, many laws created to defend guardian hierarchies (such as hereditary aristocrats and their rights in property) gave way, at the end of the 1700s, to those protecting the rights of individuals, regardless of rank or class. By the nineteenth century, this struggle was waged mostly in markets (largely in the form of contract law) and the institutions of representative democracy. By the late twentieth century, identity groups and special interests—especially economic cartels—had co-opted many of these rights to serve their own purposes. The result has been a flood of "judicial activism" that both conservative and liberal guardians attack or applaud, depending on whose ox is being gored. By the early twenty-first century, many courts no longer arbitrate disputes under the law, but have become a very streamlined and relatively low-cost way of making law—even influencing the course of major elections, as in the hotly contested presidential election of the year 2000. In this instance, the decisions of an arguably partisan Florida state supreme court were reversed by an equally partisan U.S. Supreme Court, giving the presidency to a candidate who had lost the nation's popular vote. While no real corruption was alleged, the losers complained that the winner "stole" the election (meaning he won it undemocratically) while the winners said the system worked the way it was designed. Both, of course, were right because the system—especially the archaic Electoral College—is designed to be undemocratic.

Most political guardians have come to depend on judicial activism to protect and advance their programs—some more openly than others. Even before the 2000 Florida election debacle, California governor Gray Davis a public guardian for most of his adult life, startled observers by unashamedly declaring that the judges he appoints "...should reflect my views. They are not there to be independent agents," complementing an earlier statement that the job of the state legislature is "to implement my vision."[41] According to California's chief political guardian at the time, apparently, *l'etat c'est moi*. Such attitudes not only politicize the legal system, they also make the political system itself more litigious—less trustworthy and less trusted.

In the Gilded Age of America's industrial robber barons, economic arch-guardians like Andrew Carnegie and Henry Lee Higginson knew that the demos could not be held at bay indefinitely by legalisms and social palliatives. They believed that the proper administration of wealth was the central problem of their day and that, simply because a citizen

---

41 Washington Bureau. "Davis Wants His Judges to Stay in Line," *San Francisco Chronicle*, March 1, 2000.

held title to a property, he could not do with it as he pleased. Along with other philanthropic leaders, they concluded that the ideals of service, stewardship, and cooperation should guide a community's decision about what to do with its resources. Such views challenged the classical theory of markets, including the theory of rents, that had guided judicial realism up to that time. They acknowledged that, historically, all civilizations eventually face a crisis due to the need for land reform—to reconcile domain with dominion.

America postponed that crisis for almost two hundred years by annexing new territory, expanding opportunities for home ownership, and then—when all else failed—extending certain rights traditionally associated with property to non-propertied citizens. However, none of these "solutions" have thrived in the economic and political order of the twenty-first century, which includes the rapid growth of multi-cultural populations and the expansion of global corporatism—developments that have caused many to wonder if there isn't a better, fairer, and more natural way for human beings to govern themselves.

9

The Democratic Personality

BEHAVIORAL SCIENTIST ARTHUR DE VANY marveled at the power of decentralized decision-making when he noted how a huge crowd can empty a stadium in minutes, solving a complicated mathematical problem without any central direction.[42]

Such decentralized processes are found everywhere in nature, including the human body. Our immune, digestive, endocrine, and autonomic nervous systems take pretty good care of themselves, alone and synergistically, without conscious direction from anyone. Even at the cellular level, each neuron takes a "vote"–tallies the input from thousands of dendrites until a critical mass is achieved–before acting on a particular signal. Social animals like ants, undoubtedly one of the planet's most successful life forms, have developed heterarchy (decentralized cooperation among co-equal groups), to an instinctual high art. Internet guru Steven Johnson even gives this art a name: *emergence*, which he characterizes as "...complex adaptive systems" that move from "low-level rules to higher-level sophistication."[43]

Still, most of us Homo sapiens willingly place our political and economic trust in one or a few guardians rather than taking matters into our own hands. Why should this exception to one of nature's most pervasive

42 "In an On-Line Salon, Scientists Sit Back and Ponder 'What Is the Question You Are Asking Yourself?" *New York Times*. December 30, 1997.

43 Johnson, Steven. *Emergence: The Connected Lives of Ants, Brains, Cities, and Software*. New York: Scribner. 2001. 18.

rules prove so seductive to the species that, above all others, should know better?

Civilization itself gives one clue. Humans act together to achieve individual and collective good, but so does a colony of coral when it forms a reef. Not all social animals (least of all, ants) have culture, and not all culture leads to autonomy. We may have democracy in our genes, but realizing its potential depends a lot on our environment. Do guardians and democrats create, or are they created by, the culture that surrounds them?

One answer lies in a closer look at hierarchy: not just the power hierarchy of guardians, but also the pyramid of values and beliefs that lead to participation.

Hierarchies are everywhere. They include natural categories like predator and prey, young and old, healthy and sick; but they also include such socially constructed categories as experienced and inexperienced, mature and immature, aggressive and restrained, knowledgeable and ignorant. When it comes to guardianship, we learn first from our parents the importance of power hierarchies. Mom or Dad, or both, make big decisions, and when they're not around, the older look after the younger siblings. From our peers, we learn to redistribute that power into new pecking orders based on all kinds of useful criteria: from size and strength to intelligence and wealth. Once we experience the perils of subordination and the joys of being on top, many of us develop a taste for dominating others—especially when those hierarchies are exploitative, as those created by immature people often are. Economist Robert Hielbroner calls these childhood hierarchies, "...the great readying experience that prepares us for the adult condition of sub- and superordination," a system of domination so natural that we seldom question its guilty pleasures and stultifying consequences. "Infancy," he says, "is the condition from which we must all escape, and as such, the source of the emancipatory thrust that is also part of the human drama."[44]

Self-emancipation, ultimately, is what maturity is all about; and far from excluding hierarchy, it specifically embraces those hierarchies that encourage self-determination. Valid hierarchies support our human drive for individualism within a social setting. They promote our ability

---

44 Heilbroner, Nature and Logic.

to participate in consequential matters and help others participate, too. Remember, the opposite of hierarchy is not perfect equality, but chaos—and neither guardians nor democrats seek that. Invalid hierarchies stifle consent, limit participation, and suppress that "emancipatory thrust" that leads to self-governing societies.

Fortunately, as we mature, our capacity for mutual cooperation increases dramatically. Over millennia, universal coercive guardianism gradually yielded to institutions that encourage self-direction. Kin-based tribalism gave way to despotism, allowing coordinated action among unrelated groups. Despotism yielded to monarchy, wherein a king rules with the consent and cooperation of a hereditary aristocracy. Monarchy has since been replaced in most parts of the world by representative democracy: guardianship by elected aristocrats. Individually and collectively, each step away from the presumed parental authority of one adult over another brings us closer to the goal of universally shared autonomy: the replacement of invalid with valid hierarchies.

This progress (and we really must call it that) works like artificial selection in biology. Over the very long haul, the slow mutation of our social systems has cultivated what we might call an empathy reflex, or has made dominant a somewhat recessive—and thoroughly metaphorical—"fairness gene" that leaves groups of well-socialized individuals better off than those who never rise above tribal parentism or despotic guardianism.[45]

The great implication of this is that humanity has steadily required fewer coercive institutions to protect people from themselves. Instead, cultural evolution has increasingly favored institutions that allow our naturally sociable, empathetic, and self-directing nature to assert itself. And the more we practice such skills, the better we get at them, making coercive guardianship less useful and eventually maladaptive. Just as important, our in-born drive for collaborative self-direction creates an implicit

---

45 Research in an expanding field called "experimental economics," in which classical assumptions about large- and small-scale social and economic behaviors are put to the test, suggest that in most cultures, "people value fairness highly and emotionally" and act far less selfishly and much more cooperatively than previously assumed; the product of millions of years of evolution that "prompt us to behave in ways that would have benefitted either us or our group in the long run." (Sigmund, Karl; Fehr, Ernst, and Nowak, Martin A. "The Economics of Fair Play," *Scientific American*, January 2002.)

expectation that we will eventually achieve it—an expectation that, when widespread enough, will eventually be perceived as a human right.

At this point one might reasonably ask, "What if an adult genuinely believes that guardianism is good, is in accord with human nature, and that its institutions do allow people to grow personally while partaking in a meaningful economic and political life? Wouldn't that make guardian hierarchies as valid as any other?"

Such beliefs are not only understandable, they are commonplace—as the long age of guardianism proves. Unfortunately, widespread belief has never been the acid test for truth, as members of the once-flourishing Flat Earth Society can attest. Guardian hierarchies lack validity because their processes, by definition, are exclusionary and nonconsensual. As long as even one person realizes that involuntary guardianship is a barrier to his or her further growth as a human being while guardianship is still forced upon him, the hierarchy enforcing it is invalid.

This distinction is more than semantic. In a self-governing, free society some people may decide to adopt guardians if they wish—to give their political or economic "power of attorney" to someone they think is better qualified to exercise those rights—but only for themselves. Under compulsory guardianships like representative democracy, the option of true self-determination is reserved only for those citizens who are willing to deny it to others; namely, those who join the guardian elite. Guardians must always exclude and threaten coercion, or they cease to be guardians. Democrats must always include and seek consent or they cease to be democrats.

Most of all, socialization in a civilized culture is not a passive activity. Like individuation, it requires exploration, introspection, and a realistic understanding of the world. This increased knowledge about one's self and others leads to increased self-confidence and mutual trust. Trust, in turn, leads to more openness and interdependence. When reciprocated, this deeper engagement among people results in tolerance, self-restraint, and a true sense of community—even civic friendship. Because guardianship is exclusionary, it short-circuits this natural process just as it begins: when maturing adults finally decide they are ready to make joint, binding decisions about the things that matter most.

Ultimately, this biological and psychological drive toward collaborative autonomy is perhaps the most powerful engine we have for the preservation, growth, and advancement of our species. Everyone possesses this capacity to some degree and it only gets stronger with use, as we find new opportunities to convert our better instincts to experience. In this way, direct participation, like a fusion reactor, creates its own "fuel" even as it releases new energy. Just as human embryos mimic the stages of human evolution on their journey from conception to birth, so do we—individually and collectively—pass through stages of our shared social evolution as we mature from children to adults.

What makes a democratic personality? We might as well ask what makes a competent adult? Guardians may aspire to become philosopher kings, but democrats only want to grow up—to fully realize the potential that nature placed within us.

10

Three Myths about Participation

OVER THE YEARS since America's founding, and especially in recent decades, Americans in the millions have joined support, service, affinity, and advocacy groups of every kind, not just to recoup a sense of community lost after generations of guardian rule and an anonymous consumer culture, but to find meaning and coherence in their daily lives. Research by Princeton sociologist Robert Wuthnow shows that such groups arise mainly because the individuals involved felt "the desire to grow as a person"–to achieve those final steps toward full adulthood that promotes autonomy within community.[46]

This "off-the-books" (outside formal political and employment channels) approach to citizenship brings with it several problems. Although it allows people to deal directly with each other in small-scale, community matters, it also reinforces three very powerful–and very false–myths about direct participation that are happily promoted by most guardians.

The first myth is the belief that any sort of direct political or economic participation requires face-to-face interaction. This means that the demos, or voting population involved with the issue at hand, must be small enough to permit personal interaction among all participants. This belief is owed largely to our experience growing up in families, interacting in classrooms, and earning a living in small work groups. It also matches our experience with committees, clubs, professional associations, and other ad

---

46 Wuthnow, Robert. *Sharing the Journey: Support Groups and America's New Quest for Community*. New York: The Free Press. 1994.

hoc groups where "things get done." It's consistent, too, with the practices of the ancient Greek city-state, whose demos met in the agora, or public square, and the Roman Republic, whose citizens assembled in either the Forum or the Field of Mars outside the city gates. It is also the model of participation held up to us by modern guardians because that's the way they supposedly do business: on the floor of Congress and in state legislatures, during Presidential cabinet meetings and in corporate boardrooms. Why, then, is this time-honored and widespread experience a myth?

First, real communication within these groups–the detailed interaction that sets agendas, defines problems, crafts alternatives, frames decisions, and makes deals–actually takes place through many other channels, virtually none of them "in the agora." Only the voting itself occurs with all members present, and even then most communications are procedural, ceremonial, or intended for outside consumption, such as remarks "read into the record" to document dissent or please constituents. As a result, most voting participants have already made up their minds about the issues involved–in other words, they have already deliberated–before the assembly is convened. Although records of stirring public debates and dramatic (even violent) elections abound, this practice was as true in antiquity as it is in modern parliaments and legislatures, where political deals are routinely hammered out in committee, on the phone, through e-mail, or by power brokers working behind closed doors.

This myth was alive and well at the Constitutional Convention of 1787. Anti-federalists thought direct self-governance by Americans was desirable but impractical due to the country's great size, as indeed it had been even at the state level before the revolution. Still, numerous delegates sounded dire warnings about the dangers of representation. New York's governor George Clinton warned his delegation to avoid any system that installed representatives who, "possessed of all the powers of government, and who, from their remoteness from their constituents, and necessary permanency of office, could not be supposed to be uniformly actuated by an attention to their welfare and happiness..."[47] Two members of the South Carolina delegation were even more critical of national guardianism, pre-

---

47 Bailyn, Bernard Ed. *The Debate on the Constitution, Part 2.* New York: The Library of America. 1993. 4-5.

dicting that, "...everything would be managed in future by great men, and great men everybody knew were incapable of acting under influence of mistake or prejudice...so that if at any future period we should smart under laws which bore hard upon us...the answer would be–Go, you are totally incapable of managing for yourselves with public concerns–mind your business–"[48]

Federalists, on the other hand, were adamant about keeping real power in guardian hands "to the exclusion of the people in their collective capacity," as James Madison so bluntly put it.[49] Thus, applying to public issues the skills, insights, and problem-solving methods the vast majority of us use every day in private life was reserved from the beginning for "our betters" simply because, every once in a while, they could all fit into one room.

Today, most people (including guardians) will admit after reflection that a face-to-face encounter–especially in the presence of strangers–is often the worst way to achieve high-quality communication, let alone an understanding of complex issues or to examine alternatives and make reasoned choices. This is why face-to-face encounter is advocated mostly by the people who do it best: those skilled in oral communication, adept at advocacy, and psychologically motivated to dominate any group–in short, natural guardians. Such people have an advantage in face-to-face encounters, which is one reason they run for office, volunteer for committees, and seek opportunities for public speaking. When a group gets much bigger than the number of people who can comfortably sit around a kitchen table, dialog too often becomes diatribe, and personality takes over from polity. Views aren't just presented, they become positions that are defended ferociously out of a fear of losing face. Just as bad, less-skilled communicators often clam-up defensively or go out of their way to conform to group norms, regardless of their real feelings, just to avoid embarrassment or socially awkward conflict. This is one reason the city of Berkeley, California–long known for its contentious public

---

48 Ibid.
49 The Federalist, Number 63.

hearings–established a virtual town hall on the Internet, specifically to draw less-vocal citizens into public debate.[50]

This myth is also where the "tyranny of the mob" originates. Nazi brownshirts smashing windows on *Kristallnacht*; plebeians storming Rome's granaries; youth gangs burning stores in South Central Los Angeles; night riders lynching blacks in the American south–all these began with "people publicly assembled," but not with an inclusionary, participative, democratic intent. They were an assembly, to be sure, but they were not the demos. There may have been voters among them, but their intention was not to vote. Their goal was to keep something for themselves–access to resources, political suffrage, a way of life–by denying it to someone else: the very definition of guardianism. There can be no rabble without rabble-rousers; and the demagogues who rouse them know only too well the power of factions. Citizens quietly considering, or even debating, ballot initiatives in living rooms, at computer keyboards, in office buildings, or in coffee shops are not motivated to destroy the societies they seek to improve. Being a self-governing citizen means doing one's homework: gathering information as part of the deliberation process, testing one's views, and being willing to change one's mind–a little or a lot–over time. This is difficult or impossible to do after one has already taken a strong position in front of other people.

This "myth of the agora" has also been exploded through a century's worth of successful citizen initiatives held in a number of populous states. It has also dispelled a corollary notion that representative government can, in any meaningful or lasting way, unite the demos. This is because representation is inherently a process of division. It separates voters into districts, creating an "us versus them" mentality. It encourages gerrymandering and promotes pork-barrel traffic. At minimum, it creates a two-tier citizenship: one class for elected guardians, who enjoy the full rights and prerogatives of direct participation; and a second, lesser class for their dependents, who do not.

Political parties, invented for the convenience of guardians, further divide and polarize people. They emphasize differences, not shared goals

---

50 Holtz, Debra Levi. "Berkeley Residents Can Take Action on Internet," *San Francisco Chronicle*, February 22, 2000.

and values. They best reward guardians most skilled at exploiting such differences–those who mobilize interest groups and demonize their opponents while penalizing more flexible candidates who emphasize consensus.

This divisive aspect of guardianism, made worse by our irrational insistence on face-to-face interactions and one-time, win-lose, majority-rule contests as the acid-test for democracy, has caused untold damage throughout history. All republics thrive on establishing and maintaining mutually antagonistic groups, each with the goal to protect their own interests by keeping certain guardians in power (and certain preferred groups on top) while denying the apparatus of power to their opponents. Coalitions among these antagonists may form from time to time, but they seldom last and are still aimed at keeping guardians in power, not increasing public participation.

Obviously, this sort of unity is a sham. Indeed, it's been said that representative elections suppress popular will better than martial law, since elections flatter voters by making them feel essential to the governing process and not at its margins. Tocqueville saw through this charade as soon as he touched American soil, noting that in our youthful republic, government power increased the more our people perceived it to be responsive. "What citizens initially believe to be reins," he said, "...become the ends of their own chains"[51]: a yoke of obedience guardians have always been eager to place around our necks whether face-to-face or at a distance.

The second great myth about direct citizen participation is that it is capable of handling only small, easily managed problems while only guardians can address big issues.

This view is based partly on guardians' belief in their own press releases. A very small representative body called the U.S. Congress–preoccupied as most guardians lawmakers are, with short-sighted legislation designed to benefit one preferred group over another–routinely tackles problems of enormous scale. Occasionally their programs benefit the entire demos, though these outcomes may often be attributed to factors beyond guardian control, including random chance. When guardians' big schemes fail or produce unintended consequences, they blame political opponents or

51 Ginsberg, Benjamin. *The Captive Public: How Mass Opinion Promotes State Power.* New York: Basic Books. 1986.

an uncooperative public. Despite this spotty track record, they insist that the citizens who challenge these mistakes and miscalculations are incapable of doing better. Obviously, there are some conceptual and historical problems with this argument.

First, representatives are drawn from the same population they represent. Other than general requirements about age, residency, citizenship, and the like, there are no special qualifications for elected guardians–nothing, at least in the eyes of the law, that makes this "elite" so elite: they become so only after election. Even then, the skills they develop as legislators come from the democratic education they receive while practicing the legislator's art. They also receive a lot of help from government and private-sector advisors, and there is no reason to suppose that, given the same mandate and assistance, citizens themselves could not do as well–and, as we'll see shortly, many reasons to suppose they would do better.

Second, also defying logic, the representative system requires guardians to be elected by the same population it judges, after election, to be incapable of making political decisions, no matter what the scale. While some representatives may be highly qualified in one or a few areas, no person (guardian or not), can be omniscient. Said another way, if the world is too complex to be understood by the entire demos, which comprises 100 percent of the electorate, how can a representative body drawn from it be more competent than the whole?

As it turns out, candidates for representative office do tend to be over-qualified in two key areas: their desire to dominate others and their dissatisfaction with the "ordinary" (that is, undemocratic or dependent) way of life. They are also under-qualified in what should really be the key component in a democratic personality: a passionate belief in the people. Just as the seeds of "mob tyranny" are sewn by factionalization and opportunistic guardians, so are the seeds of guardian abuses planted in the mechanics of a system that attracts fundamentally anti-democratic people to high office.

In a debate with Alexander Hamilton during New York state's Constitutional Ratification Convention, Melancton Smith, a fervent anti-federalist, foresaw nothing but problems with a government built around elected representatives. "I am convinced," he said, "that this Government is so constituted, that the representatives will generally be composed of the first class in the community...and if the government is so constituted as to admit but few to exercise the powers of it, it will, according to the natural course of things, be in their hands...the stile [sic] in which the members live will probably be high–circumstances of this kind, will render the place of a representative not a desirable one to sensible, substantial men who have been used to walk in the plain and frugal paths of life."[52]

These great men, Smith added, would combine to help one another secure election and other benefits, while ordinary people, preoccupied with the stuff of daily life, would find such conspiracies difficult and unnatural: "...their divisions will be promoted by the others. There will be scarcely a chance of their uniting, in any other but some great man, unless in some popular demagogue, who will probably be destitute of principle. ...the government will fall into the hands of the few and the great. This will be a government of oppression."

Smith went on to point out that average citizens ("those in middling circumstances"), being used to living within their means and "setting bounds to their passions and appetites," would be disposed more to moderation than excess and be "of better morals and less ambition than the great." Great guardians, he warned, lack true empathy for the average person and, although sharing many of their foibles and weaknesses, still feel themselves above their constituents–as indeed they are, given their monopoly on state power. In the end, he said, "...If this government becomes oppressive it will be by degrees: it will aim at its end by disseminating sentiments of government opposite to republicanism; and proceed from step to step in depriving the public of a share in the government."

In his book, *The United States of Ambition*, Alan Ehrenhalt confirms that most career politicians become power junkies because the system–the very mechanism Smith warned us about–demands it.[53] To get the contacts they need among political gatekeepers, a guardian's "public service" often begins at an early age, frequently on the staff of other career politicians. By the time they have the resources and connections to run a successful race, they have little on life's resume beyond a history of attending

---

52 Bailyn. *The Debate on the Constitution, Part 2.* 760-761, 764.

53 Ehrenhalt, Alan. *The United States of Ambition: Politicians, Power, and the Pursuit of Office.* New York: Times Books/Random House. 1991.

the right schools and joining the right organizations, political toadying and personal "gofer-ing," image polishing and issue manipulation, spin doctoring and media management. For them, winning is everything–not because they have an overriding sense of social mission, but because they simply have no plow to go back to. Most find natural allies in the career bureaucracy and think nothing of using public resources to further their interests or the interests of preferred individuals or groups, or of mobilizing taxpayer resources to sway specific elections.[54] Through the odious and clubby practices of "add-on" voting, "ghost-voting," and after-the-fact vote switching, many representatives do not even deliberate or cast votes on the bills they've been empowered to decide.[55]

University of Maryland professor James Glass studied the psychology of professional politicians and compared it to the inmates of a Maryland psychiatric hospital. He concluded that "the raw, primitive, archaic quality of the schizophrenic experience demonstrates how power works."[56]

An impulse to tyranny begins when individuals with psychotic tendencies try to insulate themselves from threats. They justify their arbitrary decisions and self-dealing as self-defense, though those acts are done made mainly to placate their inner demons. While he doesn't claim all politicians and their followers are psychotic, their collective actions can lead to a kind of mass psychosis, wherein entire societies, or substantial segments of it–such as Nazi Germany–behave as if they were. Presumably, less dysfunctional guardians would lead a nation into a slightly less crazy

54 Examples of this abound in the "B section" of big-city newspapers, including: "Lame Duck Mayor Turns Bank Robber," *San Francisco Chronicle*, December 29, 1997; Williams, Lance, "Mayor's Aides tapped tenants for 49er votes," *San Francisco Examiner*, December 28, 1997; Sahagun, Louis, "Arizona Governor Convicted: He leaves office today, faces years in prison for fraud," *San Francisco Chronicle*, September 4, 1997; Asimov, Nanette, "School Board Chief Lags in Child Support: SF official, a parental responsibility advocate, owes $5,000," *San Francisco Chronicle*, May 12, 1997; Associated Press, "House GOP Official Admits a Mistake: He handed out PAC checks on the floor," *San Francisco Chronicle*, May 11, 1997.

55 Lucas, Greg. "Not All Votes Are Created Equal," *San Francisco Chronicle*, May 9, 1999.

56 Glass, James M. *Psychosis and Power: Threats to Democracy in the Self and the Group.* Ithaca, NY: Cornell University Press.

condition, but the difference is only one of degree. This is not the promise made to us by our constitution or by the guardians who want to rule us.

In a way, the modern electoral process is enough to drive any guardian crazy. Candidates must first obtain the blessing of party gatekeepers, whose primary motive is perpetuating the party and increasing its power, not determining the common good and achieving the general will. After that, approved candidates must abase themselves before the same public they distrust and that they hope, after election, to rise above. Often in such campaigns, it's easier to lower one's opponent than to elevate one's self, so electoral contests become increasingly adversarial, ignoble, and sensationalistic. A few candidates may finish the process feeling, in some twisted but righteous way, entitled to abuse or loot the office it has cost them so much to win. They become not the benign philosopher-kings envisioned by Plato, but sociological gangsters adept at brokering deals among factions, intimidating opponents, and extorting favors—hardball politics by any other name.

This is not a new problem. It has plagued every republic in history. Mill suggested that constituents might resolve the situation not by throwing the rascals out, but by instructing their representatives on how to be a delegate and not a despot—turning them into a mouthpiece for local beliefs about the common good and general will.[57] Still, Mill acknowledged that as long as representatives are allowed to vote as they please, that's exactly what they'll do. Indeed, Roger Sherman successfully argued against putting the "right to instruct" a representative into the Constitution, since it would effectively cancel the new Congress's power to act as guardians.

In any event, the term-limits movement of the early 1990s—a bandwagon onto which many guardians themselves eventually hopped—was, perhaps, the first public acknowledgment by officials that guardian exceptionalism was a myth. Many states felt that representation had inappropriately become a lifelong profession and set limits on how many times its "most knowledgeable" guardians could be re-elected. Still, to most career politicians, killing time between different elective offices

---

57 Mill, John Stuart. *Three Essays: On Liberty, Representative Government, The Subjection of Women.* New York: W.W. Norton & Co. 1975.

meant a temporary stint as an appointed official, campaign advisor, or lobbyist. Hardy as rats and roaches, even unemployed guardians are as tenacious in their claims to superior rights as the old French aristocrats were in theirs.

The idea that a handful of people can ever be better than all of us at handling society's problems, large or small, reveals two fundamental failures in guardian reasoning. First, by limiting our choices to candidates who, because of their distaste for private life, need to dominate others and willingness to collaborate with an inherently anti-democratic process, we consistently select the worst possible people to be our guardians. Second, by limiting true democratic participation to a tiny fraction of the legitimate demos, we deny ourselves the problem-solving resources and collective life experience of our own great numbers. Guardians who argue that the best people generally do run for office overlook the fact that these same capable people would not be excluded from participating in a more broadly based, direct democracy–in fact, their contributions and leadership would be sought, valued, and welcomed; they would simply be prevented from denying that same participation to others.

This raises the collateral question of "expertise." Are we better off consigning complicated problems to guardians who represent themselves as, or are acknowledged to be, experts in a certain field, or should we handle these problems ourselves using the total resources of the demos, which includes the advice of experts? Here, too, logic and experience provide the answer.

By devoting a large chunk of their lives to mastering one field, experts necessarily forego comparable experience in others. They become less knowledgeable about many things while seeing a few things as disproportionately important. Even when consulted about matters in their field, they tend to take the world view of one profession, and their "solutions" have an uncanny way of depending on, and increasing, the power and centrality of that perspective. What's worse, research suggests that "incompetent experts" are more common that we suspect. In a study published in the *Journal of Personality and Social Psychology*, professors David A. Dunning and Justin Kruger discovered that the hallmark of incompetent people appears to be blissful self-assurance. "Not only do they reach erroneous conclusions and make unfortunate choices," Kruger says, "but their incompetence robs them of the ability to realize it."[58] Remember that the next time your favorite representative campaigns on the slogan that he or she is "the best person for the job."

It's no wonder then that the source of much of the vaunted complexity in our political economy comes from the myopic, solution-specific way these experts frame the questions our laws must answer. In reality, most social problems encompass many factors, and the wider the range of experiences we bring to bear on them, the better our solutions will be.

The final myth involves the way guardians have conditioned the demos to view itself. While making minute distinctions among competing candidates, guardians and their boosters try to lump all voters together, assuming conveniently that the lowest common denominator is the most relevant voter statistic. Since public opinion often follows a bell-shaped curve, guardians claim that the "highly informed" votes of the educated elite fall at one tail of the curve only to be canceled out by the votes of dullards and dropouts at the other, leaving most decisions to the great, mediocre middle. They forget that voting is a voluntary act, and that ignorant, apathetic, and alienated people generally don't go to the polls at all, making that "mediocre middle" a bit more knowledgeable and involved than guardians pretend.[59]

The tails of the curve in this case represent not "good" versus "bad" citizens, but opposing, extreme positions—and those do indeed tend to cancel each other out, which is not such a bad idea in a democracy.

It takes all kinds to make a world—and a demos—and the various personalities, styles of thinking, and experiences possessed by constituents really do complement each other, giving society more resources and

---

58 Goode, Erica. *New York Times*. "Incompetent People Really Have No Clue, Studies Find," *San Francisco Chronicle*, January 18, 2000.

59 Even experts have backed away from the notion that super-smart guardians make better public policy decisions than average citizens. Neuroscientist Lise Eliot notes that "Psychologists have proven that people can and do perform very wisely in certain real-life situations, regardless of their scores on IQ tests"; and that multifaceted "general intelligence," which defies conventional measurement and includes dimensions like social cooperation as well as perception, memory, attention, and categorization appears to be a widespread human trait. (Eliot. *What's Going On in There?* 394.)

choices than it could ever obtain from a limited number of guardians. After all, who knows better what constitutes the common good and general will–the raw materials of a good life, widely shared–than the people who have done, and will do, the living.

11

Selfishness Versus Self-Interest

ANOTHER ARGUMENT GUARDIANS use against direct citizen participation–one rising almost to the level of myth–is that ordinary people are just too selfish to put public interests first. Without getting too Freudian about it, that's a revealing projection: one that seems to say more about guardian thinking than our own.

Of course, we have few reasons to care about our neighbors until we get to know them, just as we have little reason to trust our own judgment until our opinions have been tested. Such knowledge doesn't always lead to affection or self-confidence, but it generally leads to insight; and, when coupled with maturity, to that special kind of insight called empathy. If nothing else, this chain of events—a true learning experience–shows that caring and involvement are not gifts from heaven or the endowment of an anointed few, but traits anyone can acquire when given the chance.

Here is where one of the biggest hypocrisies of guardianism becomes most evident. Guardians often complain that voters aren't involved enough with politics and use that as an excuse to deny them direct self-governing experience. Even when representation falls out of favor (as it periodically does, seen most recently in the term-limits movement of the early 1990s) political guardians still blame voters and not themselves for bad legislative outcomes and civil disengagement. In a survey of congressional representatives, Chicago's Joyce Foundation discovered that politicians fumed when voters insisted they take a stand on issues and then held them accountable for the consequences.[60] Representatives also complained that few voters bothered to attend their "town hall" meetings, even though they acknowledged that, as representatives, they had no obligation to act on what they heard.

In the private sector, an article from this same period in *The New Republic* shows how political and media guardians work together, if inadvertently, to keep citizens disengaged. The piece, written by *Newsweek's* Washington correspondent, Steven Walkman, titled "Too Many Choices," lists the horrors of direct citizen participation, among them: eroded commitment (the more choices we have, Walkman says, the less we value any one of them); lost productivity (civic engagement takes too many hours away from wage labor); lower self-esteem (with nobody to blame but ourselves, we feel bad–not just mad–about mistakes); diluted party loyalty (with a legislature composed of everyone, who needs Republicans and Democrats?); and reduced group solidarity (self-governing citizens are less dependent on guardian leaders to rally around). The solution to all this, Walkman claimed, is more guardianism–to further reduce those troublesome "middle liberties" that encourage people to think for themselves. These views are discouraging, to say the least, especially when coming from an experienced journalist, but that's not what makes them depressing. What's truly sad is not that Walkman would choose such options for himself, but that he wouldn't think twice about forcing them onto everyone else–the guardian creed in a nutshell.

This last problem, perhaps, is the central paradox both guardians and democrats must live with. Direct participation is not an end in itself, but a means to better things. It is the mechanism by which we citizens, no matter how far-flung or different, learn more about each other and ourselves. By assessing our individual interests, then deciding which alternatives match or transcend them, we coordinate our preferences with others and arrive at the general will.

---

60 Associated Press. "Politicians Say Public Is Partly to Blame: Anonymous replies to criticism that Congress is ineffective, out of touch, cowardly." *San Francisco Chronicle*, April 6, 1992.

While many fine arguments can be made against representation–from its gross inefficiencies (what is more wasteful than a new congress or legislature immediately repealing the acts of its predecessor?) to the many practical benefits that would be derived from a more politically engaged population–the one that trumps them all is the plain fact that widespread democratic learning simply builds a better society: one that is more compassionate, empathetic, cooperative, and resourceful. No one claims that guardians can't be competent, be fair, or value reciprocity only that by forcing their rule on the demos, they inhibit the development of these qualities in others. Content with their own "parental" rights and privileges, they refuse to let their "children" grow up, and that is the biggest tragedy of all.

12

Workplace Democracy: Can Employees Manage Themselves?

CORPORATE GUARDIANS CREATE what Heilbroner calls "a veil that obscures understanding and recognitions that, were they present, would cause 'economics' as well as market societies to look very differently from the way they do."[61] Lifting that veil, he sees a system of free enterprise that prizes freedom only for guardians and organizes work for non-guardians in very demeaning ways. It requires workers to subordinate themselves to employers in ways that not only are counterproductive, but would actually be illegal in other areas of life–particularly those which have outgrown the medieval tie to property.

Look, for example, at a typical wage-earner's employment "contract." From the perspective of property rights, wage earners rent their work capacity to the company. But this capacity is only a promise. From the guardian's perspective, work must still be "extracted" from the employee, the way gold is dug from a mountain. To the worker, the company has rented only the opportunity to receive a yet-unspecified contribution to the enterprise–one both parties assume will be consistent with the contributive standard typically applied to wages: namely, that employees will generate at least as much money as they cost. Corporate guardians, on the other hand, believe they have already purchased a certain minimum return on their wages–at least a normal profit, and hopefully much more.

---

61 Heilbroner, Robert L. *Behind the Veil of Economics: Essays in the Worldly Philosophy.* New York: W.W. Norton & Co. 1988.

Unfortunately, despite carefully crafted job descriptions and negotiated union contracts, most workers and managers don't know precisely what tasks workers will be asked to perform over the entire employment period, which can theoretically last a lifetime. Time, therefore, becomes not just the essence of a wage contract, but almost its entirety, and the potential for inequity becomes greater the longer the employer's return on wages exceeds normal profit while the employee continues to have no say in how that surplus is generated and distributed.

Now, classical economics assumes any transaction price–including the wage for labor–is based on a free-market exchange. In an employment contract, however, the price of labor is necessarily determined before the full terms of the exchange have been established. In this way, gainful employment is more like a marriage than a market transaction. The "obey" part is clear and begins on the first day; but the "love and honor" part–what the firm will ultimately rely on for an employee's loyalty and productivity—depends on a lot of things that have yet to happen. Corporate guardians assume they have rented motivation as well as capacity, and motivation is more closely associated with psychology than economics. From this perspective, real-world productivity–in fact, the whole idea of an employment contract–is really a question of emotions and politics. If we truly believe that the democratic process, even the highly flawed version used in representation, is the best way to make political decisions, why do we stick with the obsolete feudal system of "rents and fealty" when it comes to work and wages?

One reason the current system of voluntary servitude has persisted so long is the ability of guardians to control productive resources, parceling them out mostly to other guardians or to favored groups on advantageous terms. Under such terms, employee compensation can be equitable only by accident, since an unknown and virtually unlimited number of alternate uses for those resources have been foregone once they have been allocated for a specific corporate purpose, such as "hiring Bob" or "adding a new store to the chain."

This point may seem trivial or academic, but it creates many practical problems. On the job, it means that the act of work–as a way of harnessing society's productive resources–is, to use Heilbroner's terms, "inextricable from exploitation." It is an alternate way of exercising political power that bypasses even a nominal democratic process.[62] Such exploitation, while desirable from the guardian perspective, is expensive to enforce. When jobs are plentiful, employee turnover is high as workers seek more equitable compensation and better working conditions elsewhere. When jobs are scarce, the temptation to squeeze greater returns out of an anxious workforce can turn even considerate managers into tyrants. This doesn't mean today's "wage slaves" are worse off than yesterday's real slaves, only that an economy run by guardians can never achieve all it might and flunks any broad-based test for fairness.

Thus we see in guardian-dominated private enterprise the same phenomenon we saw in representative government: guardians who believe their dependents are incapable of self-direction and behave in a way that makes that fallacious belief seem true.

Most proposals for workplace democracy are based ultimately on this one central premise: that all notions of economic hierarchy–from the capitalist's contributive standard to Marx's value-added standard–must go. Work, these theorists say, must be evaluated in terms of its overall worth to society, not just its conversion to a marketable product or service. After all, a job is far more than a paycheck or one element in a product's price; it is a locus of control, a point of concentration for creative and productive human powers, a source of personal identity and self esteem. When these things are strong, workers (and the community around them) tend to be psychologically healthy. When they are weak, individuals and societies suffer.

For example, people who love their jobs seldom refer to them as "work." People who consider their jobs to be part of a larger, positive definition of themselves–as human beings and members of society—let that feeling spill over into other parts of their lives, transmitting it to their peers and children, who are then more likely to approach their own vocations with a similar attitude. If that confidence and optimism is based even in part on these people's ability to direct their own lives and collaborate with others reasonably well, then it contains all the seeds necessary for a flowering of consensual democracy.

---

62 Ibid.

International management guru Charles Handy said that "When the assets of an enterprise are primarily its people, it is time to rethink what it means to say that those who finance the enterprise can in any sensible way 'own' those assets."[63]–a self-evident truth that has two big implications.

First, since an enterprise's assets include goodwill–the loyalty of its customers, its creditworthiness, and its reputation in the community– then a corporation's roots run deeper into society than any specific expectation of profit. Further, the valuation of goodwill, like transactions in an efficient market, is a decentralized, reciprocal activity. Guardians by themselves can't command it. It makes no sense, then, to arbitrarily grant control over so important a shared asset–one with very real economic consequences–to a handful of guardians, excluding in the process the many material stakeholders who actually establish its value.

Second, it reminds us that economics is a social science. Economic activity is as much about psychology, sociology, and politics as it is about aggregate demand and market theory. It is a group-based way of making decisions and solving problems that involves myriad stakeholders, not just a tiny fraction of people who were lucky or clever or ruthless enough to monopolize the guardian function. For if a business's "people assets" are not chattel, then they must be something else; and in a democracy, they are citizen-workers who not only have the right, but the responsibility, to be self-governing.

Of course, accepting workplace democracy in principle and achieving it in practice are two different things. For consensual participation to replace coercive economic guardianism at least two major areas must be reformed: property law and moral expectations.

Many populist crusaders think that if we can only "throw the rascals out"–replace a few greedy cads with enlightened souls like themselves–our troubles will be over. Unfortunately, even a benevolent despot is still a despot and replacing bad guardians with good guardians does nothing to democratize the system; in fact, it just entrenches it more deeply by removing the daily irritants that remind people how guardianism stunts their growth. It took centuries of statutory and case law, and a long tradition of rigorous academic and philosophical debate, to create the awareness

---

63 *Fortune*, Oct. 31. 1994. 162.

we have today about property, rights, inequality, and fairness. Although many of us can imagine a better, more democratic world, most of us can't imagine it, don't have time to imagine it, and even if we did, see nothing but headaches trying to achieve it. What's more, current law is on the side of guardians, not democrats.

Thus, it is unreasonable to expect a board of directors or management team to suddenly champion meaningful democratic reform in the workplace when doing so would violate their own corporate charter and any number of contrary legal obligations. Pathbreaking experiments led by bold "Spartacus" types who rebel despite these forces are admirable and necessary to show what can be done, but their genius and sacrifice will be wasted until the deep pool of anti-democratic laws, regulations, institutions, and traditions can be drained, at least a little. In short, any new, directly participative social contract must be based on laws and regulations that do not require citizens to surrender their basic democratic rights in order to survive–to earn a living as a participant in an economic venture.

Finally, the existing legal-rational system regarding the rights of property can never be made more democratic until we rethink our moral notions about who gets what. Specifically, we must uncouple the entrepreneurial and financing functions from an automatic presumption of proprietorship. Instead, we must as a matter of course extend the tangible and psychological benefits of ownership to the other factors of production as well, not just to those who contribute the first dollar or idea. There is no compelling reason (save our feudal heritage and natural inertia) to suppose that other relationships can't pay off as well or better in motivating people to innovate and persevere; and there is much to suggest that this motivation will be even greater if we tap the enormous psychological energy released through direct consent.

The main problem with automatically linking one group of stakeholders to proprietorship while excluding all the others is that these anointed guardians can appeal to the coercive power of the state to enforce their will. Thus, when it comes to the economy, the might and majesty of the state is aligned not with democracy (nor does it mandate any determination of the common good and expression of the general will), but with guardians whose authority rests on medieval institutions of property. This may have been a good idea in the Middle Ages, but the inequities it has spawned ever since have caused innumerable ills, many of which are with us today.

Fortunately, there is a growing sense that corporate executives and government bureaucrats, as well as the boards of directors and elected officials who oversee them, are today more accountable for their acts than in previous generations, and are less entitled to the presumed prerogatives of a guardian class. Similarly, a philosophical and judicial consensus is building that "objectified" relations–that is, those relationships formalized by laws, regulations, court and political procedures, and contracts–do not exist apart from the actions, needs, and desires of the agents who created them.[64] A government may say who "owns" a mountain, and how human beings may use a particular mountain, but it can never dictate the nature and character of mountains. In the past, we've tended to confuse the permanence of the mountain with the permanence of our laws regarding them. This obscures some important truths: namely, that life belongs to the living and that while mountains (or factories or apartment buildings) don't need a moral system, people do. If we respect our moral rights as self-directing citizen-workers, our behavior with respect to property will become more moral, too; and those mountains may indeed lend their permanence to our institutions.

---

64 Gould, Carol C. *Rethinking Democracy: Freedom and Social Cooperation in Politics, Economy, and Society.* Cambridge: Cambridge University Press. 1988. 112-113.

13

Can We Mandate Consensus?

MOTIVATION IS LIKE WATER behind a dam: its potential for good or ill is enormous. According to researcher and former IBM executive Saul Gellerman, what most of us consider to be powerful motivational goals–a desire for wealth, security, status, and so on–are nothing compared to our fundamental human desire to simply be ourselves.[65] How is this thirst for self-realization related to consensus?

People often trace their satisfactions and dissatisfactions to specific economic or political circumstances. They evaluate constantly, if intuitively, how well those circumstances allow them to live a good life free of unnecessary irritants (let alone oppression) and to achieve not just bare subsistence or a comfortable living, but their personal potential. When dissatisfactions with a job or community conditions are bad enough, such people become motivated to make changes because, at that crucial point, they begin to identify personally with what they had previously accepted as someone else's problem, or a problem too big for one person, or a problem that was best left to guardians. Such people do not even need to have a good solution in mind when they begin to wrestle with these problems, only a firm belief that the status quo is no longer acceptable. Although watershed moments like these don't happen often in the life of a nation (the American Revolution was one; the U.S. Civil War, and its continuation in the Civil Rights Movement a century later, are others), the instinct

---

65 Gellerman, Saul W. *Motivation and Productivity.* Thirteenth Edition. American Management Association. 1963. 290.

that causes them–our latent desire to control the conditions of our own existence–is ever present.

John Stuart Mill identified three fundamental feelings such citizens must possess if any system of governance (and we may take this to mean economic as well as political) is to survive these periodic challenges, or to thrive once it has replaced the previous order.[66]

First, citizens must freely accept the system and not actively oppose it. They should not spend an inordinate amount of time and energy finding ways to get around what is expected in daily life. Certainly, the pre-revolutionary American colonies, the antebellum South, and black communities in the 1950s and 1960s were alive with activists anxious to subvert the prevailing socio-economic order; but Americans today also spend an inordinate amount of time complaining about, and trying to cope with, our own guardian-induced headaches: from byzantine tax codes and unaffordable health care to the soulless policies of huge corporations, to say nothing of lesser irritants like gridlocked traffic; recurring energy, financial, and housing crises; and political scandals that seem to pop up like tissues in a box. Tolerating a system is not the same as accepting it; and eventually even the longest fuse reaches the powder keg.

Second, citizens must not only accept the method of governance freely, they must do what is necessary to preserve it. This was certainly true when patriots in 1776 tried to establish the Union and in 1861 when they tried to preserve it; and few people today would seriously propose turning back the civil rights clock to the Jim Crow 1940s and 1950s. However, enthusiasm for conventional politics–as evidenced by record-low voter turnouts and a steady decline in grass-roots party membership–seems to be waning as is employee commitment to firms who today view job loyalty as a one-way street.

Finally, Mill declared that citizens must voluntarily do what is expected of them under the system–from mundane duties like obeying traffic laws and work rules to the occasional, exceptional contribution like serving on juries or in the military. Certainly, colonial objections to British "taxation without representation" and the refusal of many blacks in the 1960s to go to the back of the bus amply demonstrate this principle, just as today

---

66 Mill, *Three Essays*, 199.

few would doubt that society has become more contentious and litigious, resulting in more challenges–both subtle and overt–to previously accepted guardian authority.

In a very real sense, Mill's three levels of acceptance reflect a kind of consensus within the demos about the quality of its political and economic life, powerful feelings that seldom appear in guardian measures of success–such as rates of employment, gross domestic product, and stock prices–and it's not surprising that they don't. To most guardians, citizen-workers are little more than a resource of the state or corporation. They are seen as a source of labor, not the locus of democratic power. In guardian eyes, people perform their civic duties and obey the law only because compliance is easier than defiance and even hard-core dissenters don't want to be punished. To guardians, compliance is as good as commitment, but the two are not the same. Compliance involves going through the motions, usually to avoid something bad. Commitment involves working hard and going the extra mile in order to achieve something good. Since participation builds commitment, this distinction is crucial to a just and productive society, and it means that direct democracy–based on consensual processes–is not only possible, but necessary if our human and natural resources are to be employed to maximum effect.

A century before Mill, Rousseau formulated his own three requirements for fair and effective governance, ideas that reflect this fundamental distinction between commitment and compliance.[67] Laws, he said, must not only be enforced fairly and equitably, they must be seen to do so in order for people to trust each other and respect the authority of the state. They must also allow people to move freely from one social or economic class to another, since it is human nature to form groups and to compare the status between them. Finally, ordinary citizens–not politicians or bureaucrats–should administer as much of the state as possible. This not only minimizes the chance of tyranny and corruption, but it also encourages people to embrace, use, and feel responsible for their own civic institutions. Create this environment, Rousseau promised, and "... you would kindle in all the lower orders [in his day, anyone who was not

---

67 Rousseau. *A Discourse on Inequality.*

an aristocrat] an ardent zeal to contribute to the public welfare," a situation quite different from today's culture of conflict, victimization, and entitlement.

Before Rousseau–in fact, in the earliest days of the Romans–we find what is undoubtedly one of the first examples of government-mandated consensual participation. To replace the corrupt laws of its former kings, the fledgling Roman Republic sent commissioners, called *decemvirs*, to study the workings of Greek city-states and come up with a legal system better suited to Roman values. They returned and published the Ten Tables of law–not as an edict, but a rough draft. Despite every effort to be innovative and impartial, the historian Livy tells us, the decemvirs knew that the "wits of ten men" counted for little against the cumulative talents and experience of the entire city. They asked that "every citizen should first quietly consider each point, then talk it over with his friends, and, finally bring forward for public discussion any additions or subtractions which seemed desirable. The object was for Rome to have laws which every individual citizen could feel he had not only consented to accept, but had actually himself proposed."[68]

This very sound psychology, like Rousseau's three requirements, works equally well for economic enterprises; for a corporation won't last long if employees continually resist and undermine the policies of top management. When guardians are estranged from dependents, both sides tend to put their own interests first, and the common good is disregarded.

The key to releasing all this civic and economic energy is voluntarism: self-initiated, self-directed collaboration based on personal consent.

Some modern democratic theorists have recast these ancient principles for the twenty-first century. Dahl has proposed five necessary and sufficient conditions for practical, direct democracy–a virtual primer on consent.[69]

First, although political and economic leaders (and the media) may still influence how people vote, no single vote should count more than another. In government, this would eliminate, for starters, the Electoral College as arbiters of presidential elections–which is not only undemocratic

---

68 Livy. *The Early History of Rome*. New York: Penguin. 204-205. 1960.
69 Dahl. *A Preface to Economic Democracy*, 59.

CAN WE MANDATE CONSENSUS?

at its core, but gives disproportionate voting power to small states. On two occasions, this unequal voting power usurped the expressed will of the people, yet guardians who administer this exclusive club see no reason to change it. In the private sector, Dahl's first condition would eliminate the plutocracy of stockholders "voting by shares," which elevates dollars over people.

Second, everyone otherwise qualified to vote must be given an "adequate and equal" chance to do so. This means simply that the government must make sure economic and social inequality does not become political inequality–that the resources of property do not trump the resources of polity in the communal decision-making process. As political decisions become visibly more democratic, pressure will mount to make economic decisions more democratic, too. While consensual participation in economic decisions would not necessarily reduce inequalities in property, it would go a long way toward making those inequalities more acceptable.

Third, citizens must have "adequate and equal" opportunities to learn about issues and alternatives that affect a particular decision, at least within a time frame appropriate for that decision. This goes beyond current notions of a "free press," which protect mostly the advocacy rights of publishers and advertisers. Just as one of government's oldest functions is to ensure that markets are honest (as in the policing of weights and measures), so must it prevent one point of view, or a few privileged and preferred points of view, from monopolizing political debate. This doesn't mean that every crackpot or extremist must be given equal time in the media, only that the demos itself–not monied interests or guardian gatekeepers–should choose which schemes deserve public attention.

Dahl's fourth condition takes this principle one step further, giving the demos control over the legislative agenda: in other words, only the demos can decide what the demos will decide. This means more than abandoning censorship by guardian gatekeepers; it means that the state must provide at least one avenue for the dissemination of reasonably objective electoral information, as well as a user-friendly way for individuals and groups to make proposals to their peers and obtain binding decisions on those questions.

Finally, the demos must be constituted using the widest possible, rational criteria for citizenship. Certain people–non-citizens, for example, or those judged mentally incapacitated—may be fairly excluded, but inclusion, not exclusion, is the hallmark of true democracy.

These guidelines codify what most mature adults already know from life experience: that participation and the opportunity to consent strengthens a person's commitment to, and the moral validity of, whatever decision is made. Further, that rules and laws made through this process tend to be simpler and more easily interpreted than the convoluted, tortured language that results from guardian-brokered deals among competing interest groups. And with simpler, more straightforward laws, the opportunity for a judge to turn legislator during judicial review is also reduced.

Yet even a broad-based, directly participative system like this will not necessarily produce consensus if it depends on one-time, win-lose, majority-rule contests. To promote consensus, solutions must become inclusive, not exclusive. That is, they must seek to achieve the common good, not just the goals of one group over another's. Such issues may be decided by a single vote if consensus is near, but it may take several votes—with the results of each round revealed to all—before this point of near-consensus is reached. And consensus here does not mean a super-majority in the traditional sense (as in the two-thirds majority needed for Congress to override a presidential veto), but a majority big enough to account for all but the most radical and intransigent fringes inevitable in any demos.

In short, not only can we mandate consensus, we must if we are to harness the astonishing, transformative power of participation—but is large-scale consensus possible?

Under representation, public officials keep an eye on the economy and track the creation of profit and distribution of wealth that results from market action, making periodic "corrections" (through regulations, law, or policy) as they see fit. Since citizens did not participate in making the laws that empower these officials, tension—and eventually, antagonism—develops among competing groups, and between the governors and the governed, over the burdens and fruit of economic activity.

In this adversarial climate, both the haves and have-nots know that dominating the guardian hierarchy is key to protecting and improving one's interests, so contests among classes, special interests, and identity groups are frequent and ferocious. Few of us pause to wonder what might happen if the main focus of these contests—the representative offices

themselves–simply disappeared and were replaced with a directly participative process wherein the coercive laws these guardians and their dependents fear, and which enable them to force their will on others, could be
passed only with the direct consent (and by consent, we mean consensus)
of all material stakeholders.

One immediate effect would be that the incentive and opportunity for
short-sighted, authoritarian solutions (let alone corruption and oppression) would be sharply reduced. With direct citizen legislation–based on
gradual consensus building, not a single win-lose vote–the emphasis would
shift from competition between classes, political parties, and personalities
(or between citizens and their own government), toward proposals that
reflect the interests of all the people–or at least the vast majority–who
must live with a given law.

Such voluntarism, participation, reciprocity, and self-restraint, born
of consent, is the foundation of direct democracy on any scale. To make
it work, citizens must disavow the use of non-democratic coercion to
achieve their aims and, similarly, reject any law that restores non-consensual guardianism or that is forced upon them by nondemocratic
means.

Even though consensus, not victory, would become the new political
grail, all the conventional tools of persuasion and electioneering–scientific
polls, think-tank studies, public agency analyses, mass media advocacy
(both editorial and advertising), and so on–would continue to play major
roles in political governance. Some form of public voter information, such
as the pamphlets currently issued by states with citizen initiatives and referenda, would complement these efforts, counterbalancing, to a degree,
the always-formidable power of money. In general, though, citizens want
only the minimum information needed to make an informed decision.
The most common voter complaint heard now about elections is that
there is too much information, not too little, and that its content is too
biased and highly charged. There is nothing wrong with passionate advocacy; but under consensual democracy, partisan rhetoric must eventually
give way to messages that normalize differences and expand the circle of
consensus if a proposal is to pass. It will no longer be enough to force a
bare majority, effective only on the day of balloting, to ram preferences
down the throat of the losing side.

The raw material for consensus building, of course, is the demos itself. Advocates will no longer win elections by suborning or colluding with key guardians and energizing (or demonizing) certain groups, but by facilitating an expanding network of informed citizens who, having statutory opportunities to make contrary and complementary ideas part of the proposal, will become advocates in their own right.

As it stands now, the demos is composed of four types of citizen, each with a different level of readiness for participation in such networks.

The first category contains our current guardians. These range from representatives, elected or appointed government officials, and senior bureaucrats to corporate executives and owners of significant property. While many aspects of these guardians' lives are controlled by other guardians (they function, after all, in an integrated hierarchy), they are the people who come closest to experiencing the benefits and responsibilities of full democratic citizenship—at least in their spheres of influence. Once these upper-tier guardians see that the world doesn't end when they share their current, exclusive power with other stakeholders in their area, and experience their own liberation from the guardians above and around them, they may well become consensual participation's most eloquent advocates.

The second category is composed of those citizens who actively help the first. They are the fund-raisers, campaign organizers, envelope stuffers, signature gatherers, neighborhood canvassers, and so on: the staff officers and foot soldiers of the guardian class who do everything but exercise power themselves. This category also includes those who help our official rulers by lobbying, attending rallies, and protesting or demonstrating on cue. Beyond those who are motivated solely by specific self-interest, citizen-activists serve for a variety of reasons—from idealism and the joy of belonging to a group with a mission, to a simple fascination with celebrity. But the two things they all have in common is an unrealistically high regard for, or romanticized view of, guardians (whom they view as either saintly, civics book heroes, or aristocrats excused from normal conduct) and the expectation that guardianism will one day live up to its own promise. A few pragmatic activists understand that the system is fatally flawed—antagonistic, divisive, and destructively undemocratic—but hope that their years of service or financial support will at least earn them a chance to influence a few guardian decisions.

The third category is comprised of that sizable plurality of law-abiding, responsible citizens who vote regularly and conscientiously, but whom nobody would call activists. They are the critical mass who, despite nagging complaints about the system, quietly observe Mill's conditions for stable government, though their compliance is more a product of habit than conviction. However, their primary domain is *societas*, not *civitas*; and that's just fine with guardians and their helpers, who don't want the system bogged down with too much unauthorized thinking. Some "marginals" like these have a fairly complete and sophisticated understanding of the guardian system and hold few illusions about how the political economy really works. Others rely on received opinion and gut-instinct for each issue, though their behavior over time forms a pattern that, retrospectively, reveals a coherent personal and social philosophy that is not only genuinely felt, but held in common with many others.

Because modern guardian politics involve so many negative messages and so often require citizens to choose between "the lesser of two evils," most marginals know a lot more about what they dislike than what they favor, which gives their attitudes about participation a cynical tinge. Still, they vote, serve on juries, and occasionally volunteer with charities and service groups, preserving a sense of community that keeps them engaged.

The final category is composed of those citizens who are alienated by, and disengaged from, the entire guardian-dependent system. They seldom if ever vote, care only about those laws that affect them personally, and, while generally law-abiding, see nothing wrong with cutting legal or ethical corners provided they don't get caught. The jobs they hold are often menial, underpaid, and supervised by tyrannical bosses, which only sours them further on the system. When they receive public assistance, it is often with disdain, like surly children complaining about a small allowance. Some of these disaffecteds can articulate reasons for their attitude (often in the form of Marxist litany, group-victim dogma, or conservative scripture), but most can't hold much of a conversation about anything, politics and the economy included—they are simply too preoccupied with personal angst. Emotionally, these drop-outs resemble jilted lovers. They abandon citizenship the way heartbroken people give up dating. Still, their disaffection is a hopeful sign, because in order to be hurt, you still have to care.

When it comes to large-scale consensual participation, the last two categories are probably the most important numerically and psychologically. For most of the drop-outs and many of the marginals, the personal drive toward maturity–which always includes a community component–was arrested at some point in their development. They are not irredeemable, but they require more education and experience to become fully collaborative, self-governing adults.

Political guardians, of course, like to characterize these less-mature people as typical of all voters–of the whole non-guardian class–especially when it comes to direct democracy. These uninvolved, inarticulate, and unreflective people, they say, are proof that citizens are inherently incapable of self-government; and those few who might be capable are simply too lazy and self-absorbed to do it. Although they won't admit it, guardians think these marginals and dropouts make perfect citizens. After all, they are passive, compliant, usually obedient, and bear just about any burden–from unfathomable tax codes and arbitrary work rules to divisive (and often contradictory) laws–without acting on their complaints.

Economic guardians also depend on apathetic, disengaged employees to maintain their power–or at least get their way with minimum headaches. Although these citizen-workers often observe different standards of behavior at home than on the job, their feelings of frustration and alienation are surprisingly consistent. Their workplace behavior (which tends to be artificial, ingenuine, and deferential to imposed authority) and home behavior (which tends to be more genuine, self-directed, and insistent on reciprocity) reflect the same qualities that alienate them from political life. They consider both politicians and company executives to be phony, self-serving, and insincere while their family, friends, and neighbors are more "real." Nonetheless, these citizen-workers accept the yoke of guardianism and adapt themselves to its many contradictions and double-standards, suppressing their desire for greater reciprocity and participation. Over time, this leads them to frustration, discouragement, and the pervasive sense of impotence and dependency upon which guardianism ultimately thrives.

In short, guardian institutions do not inform, but deform, our character as citizen-workers, making it appear as though our natural appetite and aptitude for consensus, on whatever scale, is mere illusion and therefore forever out of reach.

Of course, saying something loudly and often doesn't make it true–as many guardians are finding out.

14

Can Consensus Be Taught?

WHILE OUR APPETITE AND APTITUDE for autonomy comes naturally, our ability to rule ourselves—or, for that matter, to rule others—does not. Benjamin Barber reminds us "If the young were born literate, there would be no need to teach them literature; if they were born citizens, there would be no need to teach them civic responsibility. ...schooling matters deeply."[70]

The proper object of that schooling has been debated for centuries. Rousseau hypothesized that children, like his so-called Natural Man, use freedom to promote their own happiness, even though a child's world is defined mostly by weakness and inexperience. "Children," he says, "even in the state of nature, enjoy only an imperfect freedom, similar to that enjoyed by men in the civil state."[71] Here, Rousseau links the ignorance and dependency of childhood to the final condition of citizens under guardianism. Rousseau also observed that people find comfort in collective—even authoritarian—associations when they feel hurt or unhappy, then move back toward independence when their self-esteem improves. To him, guardianism was always associated more closely with pathology than health.

Like Rousseau, John Dewey and other democratically inclined educators concluded that certain kinds of schooling produced certain kinds of

---

70 Barber, Benjamin R. *An Aristocracy of Everyone: The Politics of Education and the Future of America.* New York: Oxford University Press. 1992. 210.
71 Rousseau. *Emile.* 85.

citizens; and from these, certain kinds of societies emerged. Education that professes guardianism and communicates in the language of hierarchy and coercion tends to produce not just more (and more competitive) guardians, but passive, resentful, and opportunistic dependents. Under republican guardianism, citizens openly seek to minimize their involuntary contributions to the state, such as taxes, while choosing–just as overtly–those guardians who will use state resources most generously on their behalf: to pick, in effect, the wealthy and powerful "parents" nature may have denied them. Eventually, the self-dealing and corruption inherent in such a system pulls enlightened self-interest down to the level of gross selfishness. Citizens learn not only to tolerate a guardian class, but to perpetuate it and use it as a weapon against their social competitors. The unwritten curriculum of such schools affirms that, as Barber puts it, "...knowledge is always socially constructed, always conditioned by power and interest."[72] Under guardianism, we learn to do unto others before they do unto us.

Beginning with Hobbes, liberal democracy meant pooling private resources and using them as bargaining chips against the state. Under this scheme, democratic education meant learning to define one's interests in terms of class, position, and power, then finding allies to help impose that agenda on society. Civic republicanism, a less competitive concept, originated not with the Enlightenment but from the ancient Greeks and Romans. It holds that political education means learning not only how to identify and secure one's own interests, but to reconcile those interests with the interests of the entire demos–to determine, in other words, the common good and achieve the general will. Civic republicanism, although still a guardian system, communicates in the language of inclusion and tends to produce citizens who resist domination. They view conflict not as win-lose contests, but as opportunities to find consensus, at least among most people. Instead of fragmenting a community, civic republicanism tends to pull it together.

This latter approach, sometimes called unitary democracy or sociotropism, while putting shared interests ahead of self-interest, is not the same as socialism, communism, or even altruism–all of which can be as

---

72 Barber, 213.

arbitrary, oppressive, and totalitarian as any despot. Instead, unitary or sociotropic democrats (like Mill and Rousseau) seek to form what Barber has called an "aristocracy of everyone": a hierarchy of guardians as big as the demos itself. Jurgen Habermas suggests that civic republicans place high value on deliberation and dialogue among citizens trained in, and appreciative of, the arts of discourse and empathy.[73]

From these ideas, we can infer two principles crucial to a democratic education.

First, we must recognize that political guardianism and parenting are functionally the same—even though both children and citizens, when properly educated, outgrow their need for parent-guardians.

Second, we must acknowledge that a person's need for, and desire to participate in, collective entities such as clubs, businesses, municipalities, and state and national governments, will wax and wane over a lifetime. We are social animals, but we are not sociable all the time. How much we engage in the life of the demos, or in the life of a particular demos, at any given moment depends on our evolving psychological, economic, and social circumstances. Our education should acknowledge this reality and our institutions should facilitate those choices.

As the Enlightenment gave way to the Industrial Revolution, guardians saw public education less as a way of informing moral judgment—of preserving mainstream culture and training a ruling class—than it was a handy means for creating a skilled and compliant work force. Because educated workers are more productive, they could serve both as a source for private wealth (consuming more of the goods they themselves produced, expanding markets and profits) and as a reliable source of taxes—a big improvement over agrarian society.

Consequently, schools throughout the nineteenth century increased their emphasis on practical skills, not just on literacy and character-building for their own sake. Because of America's puritan past and the religious feelings that influenced many guardians, this education was also aimed at taming the independent spirit and subordinating individuals to higher authority. Of all the accommodations between private and public

---

73 Habermas, Jurgen. *Between Facts and Norms: Contributions to a Discourse Theory of Law and Democracy*. Cambridge, Mass.: The MIT Press. 1966.

guardians, this was probably the most pernicious. It gradually turned the education system from one that nurtured competent citizen-rulers (even if those early rulers came mostly from the economic and social elite) to an assembly line that cranked out worker-consumers and passive voters. The idea that a government of, by, and for the people ought somehow to encourage self-government dwindled into platitude.

This pattern of training and indoctrinating, rather than truly educating, citizens extended into the twentieth century. This was partly due to the influence of Sigmund Freud, who believed infantile dependency and "idealization of parental surrogates" continued well into adulthood.[74] Of course, Freud's ideas were based mainly on his study of abnormal psychology, not emotionally healthy, mature individuals–least of all those possessed of a democratic personality. Later researchers, like Carol Gould, lamented our lack of institutional interest in such subjects, namely responsible people who play by the rules and yearn for a measure of shared autonomy.

One reason educators and researchers have spent so little time studying the democratic personality is that other forms of political thought and behavior–like the characteristics of strong guardians, who need to dominate others in order to succeed–seem more relevant and interesting. Also, the democratic personality clearly tends toward anonymity. It does not seek publicity, is wary of power hierarchies, and is reluctant to put itself in the hands of others. It values the capacity for independent thought, practices reflective morality, and has a high tolerance for ambiguity and change. Consensus, after all, takes time and ambiguity bothers many people, especially Americans who like a quick fix. From this perspective, the democratic personality is diametrically opposed to guardianism, which trades on magical thinking–the idea that there is always one right answer and that guardians always possess it.

The definition of citizenship changed again in the twentieth century, due to the "psychologization" of education. Here, teachers and administrators tried to explain individual behavior in terms of reaction to social forces rather than as a reflection of personal agency. The "professionalization" of education further increased the distance between teachers and

---

74 Heilbroner. *Nature and Logic*. 21.

students, converting teachers from moral guides and mentors to jargon-spouting technicians who gloried in a new-found professional mystique. As the Keynesian accommodation took root, economic guardians and their political allies gained even more authority over school curriculums. Indeed, by changing not only what was taught in schools but also what was considered even learnable by students (self-governance was not among these), the decisions left to citizens after graduation were confined largely to job choice, procreation, consumption, and periodic ratification of party-selected candidates.

Unfortunately, the parallel system of private education did not materially expand these choices. Here, curriculums might be a little broader, teachers a little better, and classes a little smaller, but to be certified by the state, the guardians' basic message still had to be taught. The net effect was to keep both parents and students largely uninvolved with the overall purpose of education, at least in the democratic sense. Even worse, commodifying education tended to reduce learning to a market transaction, diluting its power for social transformation. It converted what should have been a fully participative dialogue among students, teachers, administrators, and parents—one that strives for consensus about educational goals and methods—into a binary, yes-no decision: if you don't like what one school is teaching, try and find another. This is a problem that even the seductive device of school vouchers does nothing to correct; it simply adds more buyers to the market. The use of vouchers by poorer families may result in a marginally better education for some students, making them better wage-earners and consumers, but it also threatens to bring down the quality of those private schools which become dependent on public dollars. Even when vouchers work, they do not by themselves affect the democratic content of education.

Fortunately, not all significant learning is confined to the classroom.

Lessons taught in school can differ considerably from the lessons learned in life. Barber observed that "As students learn explicitly from the classroom, the lessons of the larger world in which the classroom exists seep in. When the latter contradict at every turn what is taught in school, an attitudinal fissure can open up which students will experience as hypocrisy."[75]

---

75 Barber. 215.

While families introduce a child to the norms of community life as they perceive them, the child's peers and teachers often create a different impression. This is especially true when it comes to questions of personal agency. Schools profess a flattering model of government, saying that it "derives its powers from the consent of the governed," and depict corporations as places where "the consumer is king"–even though the real world of harried working relatives and frustrating brushes with corporate bosses and government bureaucrats (not to mention guardian scandals in the media) often paint a different picture. Harvard professor and former private-school headmaster Theodore Sizer marvels how, "The kid assistant manager at McDonald's in the evening [needs] a hall pass at school."[76]

Just when they feel the first, powerful pull toward autonomy, teens and young adults are most conditioned to accept the heavy hand of guardianism–a force that stunts their growth for the rest of their lives. Psychiatrist and social critic William McGrath, describes guardianism's debilitating effect on the developing psyche this way: "There is no grading without degrading...the lifeblood of mental health is self-esteem. When we are mindful of this, then both professionally and privately each of us will always discourage any kind of subordination. ...It is not just a play on words to insist that the individual does not belong to the organization or work for it. He works for himself and the organization belongs to him."[77]

Yet schools persist in teaching very different ideas, preparing us not for consensual participation, but subordination to guardianism in every walk of life. "We now know that conservative activists are quite similar to their liberal counterparts in at least this regard," sociologist James Q. Wilson reports "For both groups, a politics of principle represents a continuation of, not a break with, parental attitudes."[78] With so many forces trying so hard to keep us children, how can any of us grow up?

Fortunately, families are more than nurseries: they are also economic and political units. Good parents want their children to become good

---

76 Sizer, Theodore. *Horace's School: Redesigning the American High School.* New York: Houghten Mifflin. 1991.

77 McGrath, William B. *The Heart Does Not Speak English.* Phoenix: O'Sullivan Woodside & Co./Camelback Hospital. 1975. 120-122.

78 Wilson, James Q. *The Moral Sense.* New York: The Free Press. 1993. 106.

adults, and this can eventually put them at odds with guardians who want to preserve and extend everyone's childlike dependency.

For most of history, the traditional family unit consisted of married and single adults, plus their offspring, sharing a common abode, usually with a patriarchal connection. Typically, this extended family comprised more than one generation, and its members all pursued similar occupations. This made the traditional family much more robust socially and economically than its modern counterpart, the nuclear family. Those too young or old to work outside the home took care of each other. If one or more productive members were lost due to sickness, war, death, or incarceration, subsistence was still possible without outside intervention, least of all by the state.

Until the modern era, guardian interest in families was largely confined to co-opting its loyalties when the state needed soldiers, laborers, or minions to support a political cause or leader. Thus, in one sense, politics has always been a struggle between the centripetal force of family and the centrifugal force of state. Nationalistic and totalitarian regimes try hardest to make these pseudo-familial connections seem natural, even cozy; but the better educated the family, the harder this idea is to sell.

Still, most families are not democratic. When we feel the urge to self-govern, we must transcend parental authority—at least the kind that holds coercive power over us—and demonstrate our equality as adults. To do this, we continue to use what we've learned from our parents and parent substitutes, but with a crucial difference. Since we must now make our way among people with whom we have no kinship or assumed authority, we must cope in other ways. Extended families show us these ways through the examples of loyalty, tolerance, empathy, and reciprocity we observe in networks of peer relatives; but communities can teach us these things too, through our voluntary associations.

Today, venues for continuing and expanding this informal, democratic learning are often hard to come by. The centrifugal force of guardianism is just too strong to let our voluntary, participative associations coalesce into a meaningful whole. Our smaller, modern nuclear households have become psychological and marketing units, not vehicles for social action. When a couple marries for love and procreates—surely the most individualistic of choices—it may do so without regard for guardian preferences. Without parental patronage or supporting reciprocal networks, the resulting households become emotionally and economically fragile. Government guardians see this as a mandate for increased state surveillance and management of family life, which only increases household dependency and further weakens democratic learning.

On the other hand, the rise of the nuclear family reflects a general rise in the status of the individual as a locus of rights separate from an imposed, and often authoritarian, patriarchal or matriarchal group culture. Maturing teens and young adults see it as an avenue for independence. Because today's social contract is primarily between individual citizens and the guardian state, or between employees and economic guardians, that personal independence is often achievable, even if "shared autonomy" is not.

This has led to what Alasdair MacIntyre calls a condition of *bureaucratic individualism*: a mixed blessing wherein the liberty to make minor personal decisions is won only by surrendering the right to make major decisions to guardian experts such as managers, politicians, social workers, and clinicians.[79]

This has not had a salutary affect on children growing up under such schemes, principally those whose socio-economic status makes them dependent on welfare. Studies show that these children receive significantly more negative messages about people and society than those whose parents are better educated, competent, and engaged.[80] The guardian-dominated "nanny state" may provide a safety net for many children who might otherwise fall through the cracks, but—psychologically, at least—it makes a very cold mother.

We can conclude from all this that, in either its traditional or nuclear forms, the family's biggest enemy has always been guardians who seek to expropriate its natural loyalties, exploit its deference to parental authority, and short-circuit the demands for shared autonomy sought by its maturing members. Such guardians put the state in the role of Jesus when he

---

79 Bellah, Robert, et. al. *Habits of the Heart.* 150.
80 Eliot. *What's Going On in There?* 384.

said, "He that loveth father or mother more than me is not worthy of me; and he that loveth son or daughter more than me is not worthy of me."[81]

Ironically, guardians who tout religious principles as the glue that holds families together often use those principles to fragment families they don't like: from gay households to the extended families of unwanted immigrants. However, all such networks are potential laboratories for consent and participation, and we extinguish them at our peril. When those networks are based on religion, we must remember that all religion is based on faith, not logic. Their main contribution to democratic learning comes less from their specific ethical teachings than from the way they encourage believers to transcend everyday concerns, including the pettier aspects of self-interest, and take the larger view. If God truly resides in all of us, we have little to fear from an "aristocracy of everyone."

In the community, affinity groups–from service associations like the Elks and Masons to political action groups like Greenpeace and Amnesty International–can provide a sense of belonging and participation without the shackles of determinism and paternalism that sometimes dominates families. Many advocates of strong democracy see such "boundary spanning" groups as the salvation of the representative state. They say these buffer organizations allow citizens to act collectively and gain democratic competence–to build "social capital"–without coercion or bureaucratic red tape.[82] Indeed, many have credited the implosion of the former Soviet Union in the late 1980s and early 1990s not to Mikhail Gorbachev's *perestroika* but to *neformaly*: the thousands of voluntary grass-roots associations that sprang up specifically to plug the gap between the declining and corrupt communist state and the more liberal, market-oriented republic that replaced it[83]–although that new Russian republic quickly fell prey to

---

81 Mount, Ferdinand. *The Subversive Family: An Alternative History of Love and Marriage*. New York: The Free Press. 1992.

82 Putnam, Robert D. *Bowling Alone: The Collapse and Revival of American Community*. New York: Simon and Schuster. 1999.

83 Smith, Hedrick. *The New Russians*. New York: Random House. 1992.

all the ills of "free-market" guardianism and is arguably worse off in some ways.[84]

Like Jefferson, who believed that such "little republics would be the main strength of the great one,"[85] Tocqueville saw that a variety of these "intermediate institutions" were the key to American democracy: training camps that turned self-interested individuals into public-spirited citizens. Unfortunately, many of these boundary-spanning institutions eventually become dominated by guardians of their own. While providing a laboratory where citizen-workers can learn how to set a collective agenda and exert cooperative effort without resorting to formal or coercive authority, they also serve as training grounds for demagogues and frustrated, would-be guardians who care little for the direct participation of anyone who does not agree with them. And even when such groups avoid the perils of guardianism, their power is severely limited by law and tradition. Once they find congenial guardians to implement their programs, they become part of the problem of guardianism, not its solution.

Even worse, by providing an outlet for our participative instincts, they weaken what might otherwise become a potent force for true democratic reform. By limiting consensual action to one or a few narrow fields, they blind people to the fact that the demos is all-encompassing, and that determining the common good and general will—not winning more benefits for special groups or more resources for particular causes—is what direct democracy is really about.

Ultimately, grown children who fail to differentiate themselves adequately from their parents will likely see no reason to differentiate themselves from the even more powerful state and economic guardians who surround them as adults. This is especially true for those marginal and

---

84 According to Princeton professor Stephen Kotkin, the communist elites of the 1980s largely re-emerged in the 1990s as the business and political leaders of the new Russian Commonwealth of Independent States. "...The larger truth about 1991," he says, "was that the 'triumph' of democracy involved a bid for power by Russian republic officials." (Kotkin, Stephen. *Armageddon Averted: The Soviet Collapse, 1970-2000*. New York: Oxford University Press. 2000.)

85 Bowles, Samuel, and Gintis, Herbert. *Democracy & Capitalism: Property, Community, and the Contradictions of Modern Social Thought*. New York: Basic Books. 1986.

drop-out "bureaucratic individualists," who have learned both contempt for their childhood guardians and dependency upon managers, politicians, social workers and other authority figures. In this respect, the drive toward full maturity–for autonomy within a social setting–is not only arrested for the individual, it is impounded for generations.

This brings us back to the crucial role of education and experience in shaping moral maturity. Researcher Lawrence Kohlberg's criteria for evaluating moral decisions was not the content of those decisions–the criteria applied by most religious and political thinkers–but the process used to achieve them.[86] He was less concerned with a person's particular moral position (say, that physicians should assist the suicide of a dying patient), than he was with the context in which that decision was made. Was it based on selfish interest or social conventions? Was it the product of the subject's own reasoning, ideas received from opinion leaders, or belief in a set of universal principles? Since the validity of any form of government ultimately boils down to the morality of its processes, Kohlberg's approach has great relevance to anyone who aspires to self-governance.

After tracking his subjects for twenty years, Kohlberg found that the highest level of moral reasoning–making principled judgments regardless of personal expediency or social pressure (the kind of elevated processes our guardians say they use)–generally occurred about the age of legal emancipation: the time when adolescence and parental dependence ends and adulthood and the assumption of civic responsibilities, such as voting, begins. He also found a high correlation between mature moral reasoning and education. We may be born with moral aptitude, but we need training and practice to become "moral athletes."

One trait that distinguishes moral learning from mere indoctrination into a particular creed is that the lessons learned through experience with lower levels of moral reasoning are not forgotten when the higher levels come into play. In other words, morally mature adults feel empathetic with–not adversarial towards–other points of view, even those they deem less enlightened. This simple fact has profound implications when it comes to practical, consensual democracy.

---

86 Kohlberg, Lawrence. *The Philosophy of Moral Development: Moral Stages and the Idea of Justice.* New York: Harper & Row. 1981.

First, it shows that the main ingredient necessary for consensus–a willingness to continue processing a problem until most other, reasonable views are accommodated–can be cultivated throughout the demos. It is not a rare, God-given quality available only to the anointed few, our elected or self-appointed guardians.

Second, it shows that, like other capabilities, our capacity for moral judgment can be increased through education and experience. While this was always thought true for guardians, who traditionally receive lengthy and expensive educations, it can no longer be seen as their sole prerogative. If the primary task of education in a democracy, both in and out of school, is to create collaborative self-governing citizens, this is nothing but good news; and it means that it is not only appropriate, but necessary, to emphasize much earlier in a child's life those factors which lead most directly to developing this highest moral sense. Teaching students to strive for consensus because it is needed for a more valid and effective political and economic system does not prevent us from teaching those students about competing theories, or the rationales for conflicting policies, or the practical need for guardianship functions; but it does require teachers, and everyone else, to refrain from sabotaging democratic learning by saying one thing and doing another, such as paying lip service to participation while using exclusionary or coercive methods for real decisions.

It's important to remember, too, that altruism is not the same as moral maturity. People who place a high value on helping others can be as dictatorial and oppressive as the most self-centered tyrant. To these people, the strong–almost religious–belief that "help is trumps" can easily justify undemocratic process in the name of a higher good. Again, consensual democracy is not socialism or communism, which are both guardian systems. Citizens in a consensual democracy may opt for altruistic policies or they may not, but the difference is one of widespread, binding, and personal moral and procedural consent, not guardian coercion.

The real message here is that there is no such thing as a morally neutral political or economic decision; and the first decision any demos must make is the process it will use for making subsequent decisions. In a directly participative, consensual system, we all have the opportunity to apply our own moral reasoning before a binding decision is made. Under guardianism, we do not.

At the end of the day, we must ask ourselves: If the knowledge and skills of collaborative self-governance can be learned by virtually anyone, and if anyone otherwise qualified to be a member of a demos may potentially serve as, or become, a political or economic guardian, is it moral, wise, or natural to prevent the entire demos from being so educated and empowered? Is it any more moral, wise, or in keeping with human nature to pick a few of our number to act as our parents–even though we have long outgrown our need for parents–than it would be to keep otherwise healthy and intelligent adults locked forever in their parents' house?

If the answer to either of these questions is no, then we have sealed the fate of guardianism. Knowledge, especially complex knowledge, can't be centralized and monopolized forever, let alone in the age of computers, the Internet, mass communications, and widespread public education. In fact, the usefulness of knowledge depends more and more on the cooperation of individuals and groups networked throughout society–organs within a macro-organism–to generate, replicate, mutate, and employ each bit of information until their various contributions create something new and better. Our guardians know that their biggest asset has always been our ignorance and isolation. The longer we consent, even tacitly, to the idea that democratic knowledge should be rationed to, and practiced by, only a privileged few, the longer we will languish in the prison of our own making.

15

Institutions that Promote Consent

DIRECT DEMOCRACY GOT A BOOST in the 1600s when the English Parliament conceived the idea of the "sovereign people" to act as a legal and moral counterweight to the powers of a sovereign king. Over a century later, James Madison evoked the same principle when he insisted that the House of Representatives be elected directly by the people and not by their proxies in state legislatures, as had most of the old Continental Congress. He wanted to offset the power of the states by establishing a direct link between the federal government and the people. This was still guardianism, but guardianism lite: dependency with less hierarchy.

A century after that, America's upper house, the Senate–until then, still chosen indirectly by state legislatures–was similarly "liberated" and elected by popular ballot. That most anachronistic of all American guardian institutions, the Electoral College, however, remains. It was created because constitutional framers thought the widely scattered and largely rural population would not receive sufficient information about presidential candidates to make informed choices. Today, in the age of mass media, voters and guardians complain about too much, rather than too little, electoral information; but that has not been enough to eliminate this most anti-democratic of guardian systems.

Notwithstanding these changes, the "democratization" of U.S. politics has generally meant giving power not to the people, but back to state guardians from the federal government; this despite the widespread belief among the framers, as articulated in Samuel Bryan's 1787 essay, that government is primarily accountable to its citizens, not to other government bodies. "The only operative and efficient check, upon the conduct of administration," Bryan wrote, "is the sense of the people at large."[87] Tocqueville also warned that America would eventually become an oligarchy or bureaucratic despotism unless widespread economic well-being, pluralistic associations, popular mores, and a separation of state powers was maintained.[88] In the twentieth century, Dahl added that, "The democratic process isn't likely to be preserved for very long unless the people of a country preponderantly believe that it's desirable and unless their belief comes to be embedded in their habits, practices, and culture."[89] The biggest obstacles to this, he thought, were a fragmented demos (democratic dialog usurped by special interests and identity groups), the cult of professionalism (too many people claiming a monopoly on truth based on myopic expert opinion), and the flourishing of demagogues–egotists and coercive altruists who wield their power arbitrarily.

These forces all strengthen the guardian status quo and make meaningful experiments in direct participation difficult. They deform the popular conception of what direct democracy is, and can be, and promote apathy among the disengaged and cynicism among the active. They reduce all public discourse to the level of an auction: rationing claims against public assets that could and should be widely shared. At minimum, they make guardians very possessive of their power, because distributing real authority among a wider demos means diminishing any one group's ability to get what it wants and the power of any one guardian to help them.

Because of this, a hybrid form of participation, which Dahl calls polyarchy–the "rule of many"–has appeared as a kind of way point on the road to consensual democracy, or the rule of all.[90] Despite its shortcomings, polyarchy is still a big improvement over the rule of a few, or the one, and it is gradually working its way into many American institutions. Here are its signature attributes:

---

87 Bailyn. *Debate on the Constitution.* Part 1, 55.
88 Dahl. *A Preface to Economic Democracy.* 32-34.
89 Dahl. *Democracy and Its Critics.* 221.
90 Ibid. *Democracy and Its Critics.* 221.

First, elected officials, not bureaucrats (those accountable to the demos, not to other guardians, for their jobs), must make policy-level decisions and control their implementation. Bureaucratic despotism became a real threat under the Keynesian Accommodation, but has weakened in recent years, though some agencies, like the IRS, DEA, Department of Education–even the old ICC and the partially privatized U.S. Postal Service–have shown resistance to meaningful reforms.

Second, elections must be fair and frequent. Except for the occasional, local corruption scandal, this is generally perceived as true in America, although incumbency and the power of parties to shut out new candidates keeps representative turnover, and the diffusion of guardian power, low.

Third, suffrage must be inclusive: all adults qualified to vote must have the right and opportunity to do so. This has been promoted to the point of fetish in some areas, with multilingual ballots, voter turnout drives (including tangible incentives like food giveaways, in some cases[91]), motor-voter registration, and the soaring popularity of absentee ballots. Still, much of this encouragement is selective: confined to voter groups congenial to specific guardians and parties.

Fourth, all members of the demos qualified to vote and not excluded from a particular office because of Constitutional restrictions (such as minimum age) must have a right, and be encouraged, to seek election. Lay recruitment has not fared as well, mostly because of party gatekeepers, widespread disenchantment with guardian politics (including the sensationalistic, deep-background investigations and mud-slinging that accompanies many campaigns), and the need to court special interests. Still, lower-level offices generally have no shortage of candidates, though these people usually aspire to be higher-level guardians, not democrats.

Fifth, citizens–whether voters or not–should have a right to openly criticize public officials, the administration, the socioeconomic order, and other ideologies and beliefs that shape society. This seemingly fundamental right has, in practice, enjoyed only mixed success. While first-amendment rights are trumpeted loudly and often, mostly by newspapers and broadcasters, and more people than ever take advantage of the instant

---

91 Matier, Phillip and Ross, Andrew. "Parties, Gifts Lure Voters To Polls Early: Mayor-friendly groups hit 3 poor SF areas." *San Francisco Chronicle*. December 12, 2000.

dissemination of news and opinions on the Internet, enormous financial and legal resources are still devoted daily to shutting people up–to silencing opposing or politically incorrect views and enjoining the activities of one's ideological foes. As a result, average citizens who want to be heard discover that guardians listen best to people who obstruct traffic, block government offices, and chain themselves to trees–desperate acts that often lead to arrest.

Sixth, citizens must have not only the right, but also the means, to seek alternative sources of information; and those sources must be protected by law. Again, the growth of the Internet and cable television networks–including several devoted to news–is encouraging, but this is matched by a dwindling number of daily newspapers and the death, by merger and acquisition, of many long-established book publishers.

Finally, citizens must be free to pursue these and other rights through associations and organizations of their own, within the framework and protection of the law. Again, theory in this area has fared better than practice. As with their freedom of speech, marginal or unpopular groups are often deemed "less equal" than those favored by guardians, and they face social hostility and economic sanctions as well as legal harassment and legislative discrimination when they try to assert their rights, such as holding rallies on public land.

While we see many similarities between Dahl's polyarchic institutions and certain features of the U.S. Constitution, there are also differences. For example, freedom of speech under polyarchy is not just a "negative freedom" (to use Isaiah Berlin's term for a right which may not be interfered with); it is a positive freedom–that is, something that society not only tolerates, but encourages and enables. In this sense, it becomes a stepping stone to more direct forms of participation and consent. Under polyarchy, citizens don't participate in spite of their guardians, but because of them.

Barber believes that polyarchial institutions, already encouraged to some degree by the presence of multicultural enclaves in the United States, flourish when citizens are educated and motivated to use, and are supported by, "...a constitutional system offering to these multiple peoples a regime of democratic tolerance, stable pluralism, and mutual respect that (to the degree that the ideal is made real) can protect all these constituent cultures."[92] This is one reason the United States has become a testing ground for many participatory schemes, and a worldwide magnet for immigrants and various identity and interest groups that would be visibly suppressed in other circumstances and societies. It is one of the few countries on earth where access to guardians, if not the guardian role itself, has limited restrictions. If you have enough cash and persistence and are willing to play the game, you can literally move mountains.

One of the West's oldest institutions of direct participation–the judicial jury–is also receiving new recognition as a vehicle for democratic learning.

Despite their long history in classical Greece and Rome, and their resurrection in the Middle Ages as a means of protecting citizens from the predations of kings and aristocrats, juries fell into disfavor in modern Europe (especially in non-English-speaking countries) when alternate forms of guardianship, such as socialism, gained currency. Even Tocqueville, who admired the American jury system, was hard-pressed to explain exactly how it worked, or why Anglo-Saxons deemed it so fundamental to their democratic traditions.

English juries started off as little more than village busybodies who made it their business to mind everyone else's business: resolving disputes and pre-empting vendettas and clannish violence. Common law in the 1600s organized these irregular groups into judge-like panels pledged to render impartial verdicts in accordance with evidence presented at orderly trials. However constituted though, juries in the West quickly came to symbolize the superiority of a participative, consensual peer process over the arbitrary decisions of sole guardians, be they magistrates, churchmen, or aristocrats whose allegiance was assumed to be with the ruling elite.

This belief contradicts a parallel stream of political thought which views the democratic process as one of peer-bargaining and power-brokering within the "political class," a view that has nothing to do with ideals like shared values and the common good. In his study of citizen-jurors, Brandeis professor Jeffrey Abramson categorically rejected two modern notions that juries were mere "demographic markers" representing the interest groups from which they were drawn; and that supermajorities

---

92 Barber. *An Aristocracy of Everyone.* 147.

in verdicts (now permitted in the United States after two 1970s Supreme Court decisions) are acceptable substitutes for unanimity.[93] Both of these ideas, he claims, discourage democratic learning. The first reduces individuals to ciphers for identity groups, mostly for the convenience of lawyers choosing sympathetic jurors or challenging verdicts they don't like. The second eliminates, for the sake of expediency, the hallmark of a truly democratic process–the search for consensus.

Other critics argue that juries are less democratic than they seem. They point out that pluralistic democracy requires only a bare majority to reach most decisions, and that super-majorities–let alone consensus–allow jurors holding minority opinions to exert disproportionate control over results. Even worse, jurors are specifically excused from duty for showing the one trait deemed most important to democratic engagement: a passionate opinion about the issue at hand.

All such arguments reflect misperceptions, based on guardian lore, about the nature of direct democracy. We've already seen how one-time, yes-no, majority-rule voting is not, and never has been, the acid test for democracy. Instead, it has always been just one way among many for determining a course of action. Historically, it has been used most often to select winners and losers in contests for power–not as a way of determining the common good and general will, which on juries meant serial balloting until consensus was reached. Further, judicial "disinterest" does not preclude passion as long as that passion is for procedural fairness. Again, guardians and their boosters have trouble conceiving that a passionate advocacy can exist for anything other than a particular, partisan outcome. Radio commentator Adam Hochschild was surprised by his own pleasant reaction to juror democracy when he wrote, "What moved me most about the jury process was that it tended to bring out the best in people. ...When the case was over, we shared the feeling that justice had been done. In a world so full of injustice, there is something heartening when you see one small spot where the system actually works... ."[94]

---

93 Abramson, Jeffrey. *We, the Jury: The Jury System and the Ideal of Democracy*. New York: Basic Books. 1994.

94 Hochschild, Adam. "Jurors Weigh the Facts," *San Francisco Chronicle*, July 12, 1988.

Hoschild's experience echos the feelings of lawyer-author Stephen Adler, who says his own interviews with former jurors, "was like having a conversation with someone who was just back from Nepal or who'd just had sex for the first time. They betrayed the same sense of wonder at having been to a new place and having seen life differently."[95] Indeed, a sense of psychological breakthrough, of emotional passage, of transformation and realization of latent personal and collective power is a common reaction to jury service;[96] vastly different from the way most people feel after casting their one-time, win-lose, majority-rule ballot on guardian election day.

A movement already exists to apply the random process used in jury selection to other areas of civic life.[97] South Dakota proposed an amendment to its state constitution allowing defendants to plead guilty but submit for jury review the propriety or reasonableness of the statute used to convict them–essentially putting the law, not the defendant, on trial. This movement, despite opposition from political guardians, is based not only on moral and social grounds, but on sound statistical evidence (including Condorcet's Rule and the Flynn Effect) that decisions made by a group of diverse, educated people skilled in the arts of consensus-finding will consistently produce better results than one or a few guardians pursuing their own agenda. The key to success is democratic learning gained through democratic practice; and juries right now are one of the best incubators we have for that process–but there is much more that schools, parents, corporations, and governments can do as well.

Despite a heritage of citizen legislation going back to the 1640s, mainly in New England, the framers' antipathy to direct democracy permeates the Constitution and dominated our first century as a republic. During the ratification debate, Franklin himself pointed out that, "...

---

95 Adler, Stephen J. *The Jury: Trial and Error in the American Courtroom.* New York: Doubleday/Main Street. 1995.

96 Associated Press. "80% in Survey Found Jury Duty to Be an Uplifting Experience," *San Francisco Chronicle*, August 14, 2000.

97 *New York Times.* "State could let juries decide laws." *Marin Independent Journal.* September 22, 2002.

popular opposition to a public measure is no proof of its impropriety."[98] Rhode Island was the only state to refer the draft constitution directly to its people.

However, as America evolved toward direct election of high-level guardians, a parallel–if narrower and belated–movement began toward direct citizen legislation. During the 1800s, states such as Massachusetts, Maryland, Rhode Island, and Texas occasionally used citizen referenda to resolve non-constitutional questions. Around the turn of the century, sparsely populated states in the far west, beginning with South Dakota, Utah, Oregon, and Montana, adopted the initiative and the referendum as occasional alternatives to representation. Bigger states such as Missouri, Arkansas, California, Ohio, and Michigan followed shortly thereafter.

Plans for national initiatives and referenda in the Unites States have not fared nearly so well–though they have succeeded remarkably in other countries. Proposals for direct national legislation have been floated regularly in Congress (most recently in the 1970s) only to be quashed, usually in committee and with the complicity of both major parties. Typically, these plans (which would require a constitutional amendment) allow Congress or the president to submit deadlocked legislation to the people; and permit citizens to organize referenda on existing laws. They also allow citizens to initiate legislation based on a petition signed by a certain percentage of voters participating in the last general election. Although most proposals limit national initiatives and referenda to domestic matters, demands for a "war referenda" surfaced before World War I and again whenever a major conflict loomed–mostly as a way of defusing "war fever" among representatives. (So much for dispassionate guardians!)

Although these proposals were defeated, showing the U.S. government's lack of faith in its own people, those defeats did not stop the government from recommending, and in some cases requiring, citizen referenda to settle political disputes overseas–from Central America, the Philippines, and Southeast Asia to Africa, the Balkans, Afganistan and Iraq. As Colorado College professor and initiative scholar Thomas Cronin wryly observes, "The irony that the United States prescribed a direct

---

98 Bailyn. *Debate on the Constitution: Part 2.* 404.

democracy device for others but does not permit its own citizens the same right went largely unnoticed."[99]

Such plebiscites have created whole new nations (such as Norway's separation from Sweden in 1905 and the dissolution of the Soviet Union in 1990), liberalized old nations (such as the votes in Greece and Spain to overturn dictators), and put citizens in charge of major economic reforms (as in 1975, when British voters approved their nation's return to the Common Market). The best and most sustained example of direct legislation undoubtedly comes from the Swiss, whose 1848 and 1874 constitutional provisions permit citizens to put both legislative measures and constitutional amendments on the national ballot. Since the mid-1800s, the Swiss have held over 300 referenda and proposed more than 135 initiatives, causing some Swiss to sigh, "We vote too much"; although few complain that their system is corrupt, lacks moral authority, or holds them captive to special interests.

The history of the referendum movement in California illustrates most of the social and political forces involved in citizen legislation. Led by then-governor Hiram Johnson, Californians had grown weary of the influence-peddling and delaying tactics employed by state legislators, particularly those "bought and paid for" by the Southern Pacific Railroad, a major player in California's development.[100] Concerned citizens wanted a way to either act on their own or allow civic-minded legislators to bypass committee chairmen and power brokers and take their bills to directly to constituents.

The California constitutional amendment authorizing this was bitterly opposed by most guardians. "The voice of the people is not the voice of God," boomed one former Assemblyman, "for the voice of the people sent Jesus to the cross!"[101] Opponents called amendment sponsors socialist radicals–revolutionaries bent on overthrowing the state. However, the propositions that appeared on ballots during the first few decades after

---

99 Cronin, Thomas E. *Direct Democracy: The Politics of Initiative, Referendum, and Recall.* Cambridge, Mass.: Harvard University Press. 1989. 162.

100 Kershner, Vlae. "Democracy Gone Awry: Explosion of initiatives lets voters, not elected leaders, steer the state," *San Francisco Chronicle*, May 18, 1998.

101 Wildermuth, John. "1911 Reform Was Meant to Give Citizens More of a Say," Ibid.

the amendment was passed were anything but revolutionary. A smattering of oddball and utopian schemes–from a statewide prohibition of hard liquor and foul language to an attempt to ban vaccination of school children–were all soundly defeated, while a number of much-needed reforms, including annual state budgeting and civil service employment, both resisted by many guardians, sailed through.

To date, twenty-five states have adopted the model established by these pioneers and a renaissance in plebicitary politics occurred after the so-called taxpayers' revolt in 1978–the passage of California's "Prop 13," the property tax initiative. These acts were enough to move the author of *Megatrends* John Naisbitt, to proclaim (a bit prematurely) that representative democracy was dead.[102]

Experience to date suggests that direct legislation has worked best at resolving highly charged issues–from the death penalty, abortion, affirmative action, and gay rights to more prosaic but essential matters as tax reform, term limits, and environmental laws. This is understandable, since guardians facing these issues in highly visible state legislatures or city councils stand to make as many enemies as friends, no matter which way they vote.[103] Legislators seeking to avoid controversial votes "stay off" or "lay off" the job on the day the measure is presented for approval. When enough legislators abstain in this manner, many bills die a quiet death–without the need for the lawmaker to go on record as voting against a measure championed by colleagues or key constituents. Representatives seeking to placate noisy activists or accommodate special interests sometimes sponsor referenda, sparing their fellow guardians the pain of a public vote while allowing themselves to take the high road by "placing their trust in the people"–no matter how loathe they are to do that in other matters.

One implication of this pattern, though guardians will never admit it, is that even representatives think the demos is better suited than they are to make our toughest political decisions. When pressed, guardians often agree that controversial laws passed by popular vote have a better chance

---

102 Naisbitt, John. *Megatrends*. New York: Warner Books. 1982.
103 "Do-nothing politics: When the going gets tough, more and more lawmakers are taking a walk." *San Francisco Chronicle*, June 25, 2002.

of being accepted by opponents than those forced upon it by representatives, who are always subject to criticism for being bought for caving-in to special interests.

This is not to say that the track record of citizen legislation is unblemished, or that existing schemes for initiatives and referenda make perfect models for national participation. All the ills associated with one-time, win-lose, majority rule voting apply to current initiative systems–proving, if nothing else, that consensus building counts almost as much as who is casting the ballots. Also, in a hybrid system that combines direct legislation with compulsory representation, guardians have a big advantage in setting the agenda and manipulating the process. These devices range from the almost mandatory use of highly paid, insider initiative consultants, who exercise great power over which issues get aired, how signatures are gathered, and how propositions are worded and advertised; to guardians who use existing fund-raising networks and political alliances to promote or defeat certain issues. In 1996 alone, California's seventeen ballot initiatives attracted $141.3 million in contributions–over a third more than the entire state legislature spent to get elected, or re-elected, that year.[104]

For their part, many citizens complain that initiative ballots have become too long and complicated and are misleading. All propositions claim to be sponsored by such non-partisan, apple-pie organizations as Friends of Good Government, Citizens for a Fair Economy, and so on, leaving the average voter with little to go on when judging a sponsor's credentials and possible ulterior motives. To make matters worse, the electioneers who commodify guardian politics with slick candidate packaging and attack ads do the same on initiative campaigns: eliminating any chance of consensus by demonizing opponents, and reducing reasoned arguments to catchy slogans and sound-bites–and why not? Their job is to win elections, not determine the common good and achieve the general will.

These problems are mitigated somewhat by voter information pamphlets prepared by the state and distributed before each election. These

---

104 Howe, Kenneth. "Big Money Swamps the Ballot: Initiative industry's bankroll now dwarfs that of candidates," *San Francisco Chronicle*, May 19, 1998.

surprisingly cogent, if unexciting, documents feature a plain-language summary of each proposition's main features, a reasonably objective analysis of its probable fiscal impact (prepared by a nonpartisan public agency), arguments for and against the measure, a list of sponsors–many of whom are political or community leaders–and a sample ballot that voters can mark at their leisure and take to the polls. If nothing else, the wide use of these pamphlets, in concert with the growing use of absentee ballots (which allow voters to avoid polling place hassles), show that individual citizens can, indeed, gather information, deliberate, and come to both provisional and final decisions quite successfully without having to meet face-to-face in the same room.

Some citizens suggest that initiatives should be submitted first to the Secretary of State for a review of language, clarity, and legal implications before they are put on a ballot, giving sponsors time to remedy any of the technical problems that are often cited by opponents in later judicial challenges.[105] This review, roughly analogous to the FDA's inspection of new drugs or the FAA's certification of airliners, would not give bureaucrats or incumbents the power to veto citizen legislation before it is made. (The FDA does not decide which medicines have a market, and the FAA lets airlines and manufacturers decide what kind of planes they need.) Rather, it would assure voters that ballot measures meet the same legal standards applied to any law that is passed by representatives.

A bigger problem is the fact that some citizen legislation simply goes unenforced by bureaucrats and other guardians simply because it lacks conventional political patronage. That is, most laws are subject to an unofficial understanding, or accommodation, among key legislators, high-level bureaucrats, local officials (including district attorneys and police)–and in some cases, corporate executives–about how energetically such laws will be enforced. For example, California's Proposition 187, a 1996 initiative to deny illegal immigrants access to public schools and non-emergency, state-paid health care, was passed by a large majority. However, many school principals, hospital directors, and other public administrators who had facilities and staff in place to accommodate these clients, simply

---

105 Barabak, Mark Z. "State Voters Like Initiative process, *San Francisco Chronicle*, March 10, 1993.

refused to enforce the law even if it survived appropriate legal challenges. Opponents of the measure praised these people for their "highly ethical" stance, comparing them to Germans who defied Hitler's anti-Semitic discrimination in the 1930s. Supporters were outraged and condemned them as arrogant bureaucrats who believed themselves and their "administrative empires" above the law. Whatever individual guardian motivations may have been, this civil disobedience unquestionably revealed a serious gap in perceptions about sovereignty: who really controls the government, its agents or the demos?—and underscores how essential the perception of validity and consensus-building are to the democratic process.

In the last analysis, existing initiative systems, although widely popular (and considered by many to be more trustworthy than politicians),[106] are no substitute for a more fully democratic, consensual system. They are subject to many of the problems of guardian-dominated politics with the exception of corruption in the classic sense (it is simply impossible to bribe an entire demos), and inclusiveness—laws passed by initiative are perceived by many to have greater moral force. This situation is not likely to change as long as a one-time, majority-rule victory—not consensus—is the objective and citizen-workers are still excluded from key economic decisions.

If politics is moving by fits and starts toward more democratic participation, what about meaningful reforms in the workplace?

In a 2001 Gallup poll, one in five American workers described themselves as "actively disengaged" from their company's management, complaining that, among other things, they didn't know what was expected of them, lacked necessary resources, and were often ignored by their bosses.[107] This should come as no surprise to the economic guardians involved. In his essay "Reinventing the Corporation," Roger E. Alcaly writes "Employees, as we shall see from a variety of studies, tend to be

---

106 Gledhill, Lynda, "Ballot Initiatives Trusted More Than Politicians," *San Francisco Chronicle*, Nov. 11, 1999.

107 *Wall Street Journal* "1 in 5 Workers Called 'Disengaged'" *San Francisco Chronicle*, April 15, 2001.

happier, more productive, and better paid under collaborative or participative work arrangements."[108]

Although so-called participatory management has a long and checkered history—characterized mostly by managers misrepresenting their consultative style as participation—it was not until the dramatic success of Japanese automakers in the 1970s and early 1980s (the result, paradoxically, of participative ideas introduced by American quality-control consultant W. Edwards Demming) that U.S. industry began to change its traditional hierarchial ways to any noticable degree.

One early success was Ford's use of Demming-style work teams to design and produce the Taurus: the car credited with reversing that company's decades-long decline. The challenge, as explained by Ford's former chairman and CEO Donald Peterson, was getting workers to realize they "had permission" to think for themselves after a half-century of top-down, one-way communication.[109] This problem was compounded not just by the workers' hesitancy to trust their own judgment, but also middle management's reluctance to share the power created by their previous monopoly on information. Unfortunately, "democracy" at Ford—and in most other, similar experiments—was confined to a flattening of vertical communications and better recognition of merit. The corporate culture was still authoritarian and great disparities persisted in executive-versus-worker compensation, as well as other benefits that had nothing to do with contribution and everything to do with guardian power and prerogatives.

By 1990, while the incomes of top managers and workers continued to diverge at an astounding rate, a UCLA survey discovered that almost a quarter of the Fortune 1000 companies employed self-managed work teams (compared to just over 12 percent at the time of Ford's turnaround) and that more than half of those planned to expand their experiments in worker participation. According to UCLA professor Ed Lawler, "Companies don't change because they're nice. They change because they

---

108 Alcaly, Roger E., "Reinventing the Corporation" *New York Review of Books*, April 10, 1997.

109 Peterson, Donald E. and Hillkirk, John. *A Better Idea: Redefining the Way Americans Work.* New York: Houghton Mifflin Company. 1991.

want to make money... If it wasn't for Japan Inc., I don't think a lot of this would be happening."[110]

At an employee-run cereal plant in Georgia, General Mills factory manager Pat McNulty agrees. "It's not a social experiment," he says. "It makes good business sense. Nobody knows the job as well as those doing it. If you empower those people to make decisions, they make good ones."[111] The result, according to McNulty, is reduced costs, better quality, and greater efficiency. At its Tire and Rubber Hose plant at Mount Pleasant, Iowa, Goodyear traded its system of hierarchy, regimentation, and close supervision for an organization featuring one manager, numerous work teams, and rotating squads of coordinators, with workers determining their own raises. "Sometimes sparks fly," says Dave Smith, the plant's human resources manager. "You have to take constructive criticism, and not everyone can."[112]

Smaller firms seem more willing to experiment with radical reforms, and therefore gain more lasting success. For example, when Johnsonville Foods, a family-run sausage business in Sheboygan, Wisconsin, had problems keeping up with fast-growing markets—losing sales orders, mislabeling and misrouting products, damaging equipment and neglecting maintenance—owner Ralph Stayer responded by turning the plant over to the very people who seemed to be fouling things up. He gave them complete power to hire and fire each other, grant or deny their own raises, promote or demote themselves, set schedules and profit targets, control finances, develop new products and markets, and make capital investment decisions. Stayer says, "Everybody looks at what we're doing and says, 'God, that's kind of flaky.' It isn't a soft or crazy deal. I'm a real hard-nosed, pragmatic guy... Teach people to do for themselves, this way you get far better performance."[113]

Over eight years, Johnsonville sales increased 20-percent annually and productivity rose by 50 percent. Business consultant John Zenger does

---

110 Cohen, Sharon, Associated Press "Workers Happy to Be in Charge," *San Francisco Chronicle*, December 2, 1990.

111 Ibid.

112 Ibid.

113 Ibid.

not see this as a fluke. "Companies become more competitive," he says. "The employees...learn more skills. The more you have a sense of autonomy, the happier a camper you are."[114]

This experience applies to capital providers as well. Twenty years ago, a Vanderbilt-trained economist, Muhammad Yunus, returned to his homeland, Bangladesh, with the idea of helping that newborn country improve its economy using the latest ideas in Western banking and finance. What he found, though, was that traditional capitalist guardianism was keeping the country poor. Starving people could raise themselves to subsistence, and subsisting people could achieve some prosperity, only if someone would stake them to the paltry sums needed to start a street-corner business or tide them over a lean period. Yunus discovered that all these people needed was literally a few pennies a day to keep them afloat and generate the income needed to buy not only food and shelter, but enough trade goods to pay back the loan.

Naturally, no conventional bank was interested in funding what eventually became the worldwide phenomenon known as microloans. "The banking system was designed to keep poor people out," Yunus says. "They said, 'The poor are not creditworthy.' I said, 'How do you know?' They said, 'Everybody knows. Why don't you?'"[115] In fact, Yunnus's research showed that wealthier people defaulted on loans far more often than those few poor people who ever got them. Poor merchants were generally much thriftier and more cautious than their well-to-do counterparts, knowing quite well how to stretch a rupee. To tap this resource and solve this social problem, Yunus in 1983 founded Grameen (meaning "rural village" in Bengali) Bank, which specializes in microloans. Borrowers are required to meet weekly in small support groups to help each other solve problems and share ideas. By the end of the 1990s, Grameen granted over $1 million per day in microloans in more than 36,000 villages, and it has spread its methods to the United States. Arkansas, Illinois, and other locations with sizeable pockets of poverty use elements of its method–although here, public guardians insist that the loans be administered through "proper" welfare channels, and they usually dispense training, not cash. However, some

---

114 Ibid.
115 Ryan, Michael. "A Recipe for Prosperity," *Parade* magazine, August 17, 1997.

private groups are beginning to fill this gap, raising funds for a system of national microloans ranging from $500 to $10,000.[116]

Despite these and other small-scale successes, most people still look to big companies for cues on how to make economic democracy work, and the results continue to be mixed. Union workers at General Electric's jet engine plant at Lynn, Massachusetts asked to examine the company's troubled plan for selling generator casings–a huge breach of organizational etiquette–but came up with a new, more cost-effective bidding system that won business back from a Korean competitor. At PepsiCo, where its once-profitable Frito-Lay unit was forced to lay off employees and cut back production of its high-end products due to ferocious new competition, executives could find no conventional solution to its problems. Their response was to "push" operational decisions further down toward the factory floor.

"At first workers viewed us suspiciously," manufacturing manager Steve Smith reports, "when we said we were going to turn management of the business over to them. They only believed us after we spent a lot of time teaching them the fundamentals of our business: what consumers are looking for, how to calculate profit and loss, the importance of quality, how our plants fit into Frito-Lay as a whole."[117] At the end of each shift, workers enter information about their daily operations into computers and receive instant feedback on their progress against their goals. If the results are poor, nobody yells at anybody; the team simply gets together, figures out what went wrong, and tries a new solution.

Other participative techniques have infiltrated the corporate hierarchy in bits and pieces. These include the rise of ESOPs–pension-oriented Employee Stock Ownership Plans–through which control over companies can pass (often with the help of leverage) from disinterested stockholders to the workers themselves; and, less dramatically, the "360-degree evaluation" where subordinates evaluate superiors as well as vise-versa.

---

116 Associated Press. "Microloans Help Start Businesses," *San Francisco Chronicle*, August 15, 2000.

117 Grant, Linda. *Los Angeles Times*, "Firms' Futures Rest on More Worker Involvement," *San Francisco Chronicle*, May 4, 1992.

While these developments are helpful, they still lack a crucial ingredient: namely, a mandate for consensus among relevant stakeholders before significant, binding decisions can be made. As far as ESOPs go, most participants exercise no more control over their enterprises than conventional stockholders do–largely because they are still hemmed in by the same guardian-oriented property laws and traditions that dictate corporate governance. Because of this, corporate executives often use ESOPs for their own purposes, such as foiling hostile takeovers or controlling worker behavior by manipulating the contents of, and access to, pension benefits.[118] The bankruptcy of United Airlines ended America's biggest experiment with so-called employee ownership. ESOP advocates note that a series of fatal flaws, all aimed at placating conventional guardian managers and investors, doomed the experiment from the start: exclusion of flight attendants–the airlines most visible public representatives–from participation; inability of worker-shareholders to vote for directors; inability of employees to sell their shares until they quit or retired; and cessation of employee stock allocations after 2000, creating a caste system of old employee-owners versus newcomer "hired help." As for 360-degree evaluations and other such schemes, they are, for the most part, simply job enrichment and job enlargement devices–well-known tools for increasing short-term productivity. Since they are nonbinding, guardians may disregard them without penalty.

In short, none of these piecemeal devices addresses the much deeper and more central questions of democratic corporate governance, such as asset ownership and the legal powers and prerogatives it bestows. Participative management, as most firms define it, has become just one tool among many–including outsourcing and downsizing–for guardians to contain costs and increase profits. The big questions that lie at the core of a capitalist system–allocation of investable funds, how much surplus should be generated and how it should be used, and so on–are still in the hands of traditional property owners and other economic guardians.

The sad fact is: owners and managers really don't want to (and often, legally can't) give up the rights and privileges bestowed by government

---

118 Pender, Kathleen. "United ESOP tragically flawed." *San Francisco Chronicle*, December 8, 2002.

to owners and custodians of property, including the suppliers of capital. Without reforms in these areas, any sort of workplace democracy will always be window dressing that disguises, or complements, traditional guardian power.

What has changed because of these experiments is stakeholder expectations. The democratic genie, once out of the bottle, can't be put back. One generation's "benefits and concessions" have a way of becoming the next generation's "rights and entitlements." Most observers agree that workplace democracy, in one form or another, is here to stay and will become an ever-more-palpable force in our political economy. It has already altered certain relationships among investors, lenders, owners, managers and workers that began in the industrial revolution, and promises to change them further.

According to Claremont College's Peter Drucker, "We're in one of those great historical periods that occur every 200 or 300 years when people don't understand the world anymore, when the past is not sufficient to explain the future. We are entering a 'post-capitalist' era...".[119] Drucker sees the so-called knowledge workers of the post-industrial age as the vanguard for a new classless and non-ideological society. In his view, the old European class system from which both communism and liberalism took shape is gone. The entrepreneurial function once performed by capitalists has been largely replaced by professional managers, and the industrial proletariat by "employees who are neither exploited nor exploiters...who are subordinates but also often without bosses themselves."[120] Drucker predicts the ascendancy of a "third sector" midway between the private and public: those institutions concerned with non-profit, non-business, and non-governmental matters—a web of community-based groups that helps guide and shape these other, traditional endeavors.

One manifestation of this new, more participative era is the willingness of stakeholders to demand a voice in a firm's decisions, often using the power of "consumer strikes"—organized boycotts—as well as judicial activism to achieve their goals. Using such tactics, consumers and various

---

119 Ibid.

120 Drucker, Peter F. *The New Realities: In Government and Politics/In Economics and Business/In Society and World View.* New York: Harper & Row. 1994.

interest groups forced tuna canners to employ dolphin-safe fishing practices; induced Coors brewery to liberalize its minority-hiring policies; compelled McDonald's to replace polystyrene packaging with a less environmentally harmful substitute; made AT&T withdraw its contributions to Planned Parenthood (whose programs offended a variety of Christian groups); persuaded the state of Alaska to ban wolf hunting; and led a large pharmaceutical firm, Burroughs-Wellcome, to reduce the high price of AZT, a leading AIDS therapy.[121]

But even successful boycotts are not true participation–no more than citizens staging sit-ins or street demonstrations can be said to be "participating" in normal government. These are the tools of frustrated, excluded advocates, not members of a demos collaborating to determine the common good and achieve the general will. When economic guardians respond to them, it is not because they have been persuaded through the consensus-building process, but because they have been compelled to do so by the threat of economic loss or pressure from higher guardians. Nor is the broader base of stakeholders involved in most of these adversarial actions. They are undertaken mainly by disaffected activists who wish to advance a specific agenda despite potential costs to other, excluded stakeholders–guardianism by any other name.

The bottom line is that economic democracy can never really succeed without complementary changes in the political environment–just as democratic reforms in politics can go only so far until the daily experiences of citizen-workers consistently reflect true democratic values and practices.

Dahl describes three historical "transformations"–historic waypoints on the road to direct participation–in which these seminal changes would make their first, halting steps. Transformations one and two have already happened: the experiments of the ancient Greek city-states and the emergence of large-scale representative democracy after the eighteenth century, a process that continues today with over 139 of the world's more than

---

121 Asimov, Nanette, "There's Big Power in the Boycott," *San Francisco Chronicle*, October 2, 1990; Sietsma, Tom, "Ready, Aim, Boycott: media savvy bocotters find that high-pressure tactics can force corporate change," *San Francisco Chronicle*, February 24, 1993.

200 countries now featuring free elections and multi-party politics.[122] The third–a political economy in which strong democratic procedures are valued as highly as specific policy outcomes–may be closer than we think.

Northwestern University professor Jane J. Mansbridge, imagines that this new brand of practical, participative democracy will be based on a widespread culture of "civic friendship,"[123] under which citizens treat each other with social respect; seek consensus instead of win-lose contests; define the demos in terms of its common interests; and view both civic and private relationships as interpersonal contracts–as promises made and promises kept. When general interests conflict with specific interests, the collaborative atmosphere established by a belief in consensus will encourage noncompetitive bargaining (facilitated by mediators and citizen juries) in place of our current system of win-lose contests and its reliance on legal coercion.

Of course, such a society can evolve only after an extended period of democratic education and experience in which the lessons of participation learned in one area are not extinguished by compulsory guardianism in another. In many places and in certain ways, this process has already begun.

122 Wright, Robin. *Los Angeles Times*, January 19, 1993.

123 Mansbridge, Jane J. *Beyond Adversary Democracy*. Chicago: University of Chicago Press. 1983.

16

Life in a Consensual Democracy

ROUSSEAU POPULARIZED the term *social contract* but gave it no tidy definition. Most of us see it as any compact that spells out a process for government. Such compacts do not concern themselves with specific laws, but provide the ground rules under which specific laws are made and evaluated.

A social contract for consensual democracy would maximize opportunities for citizens to participate in framing and passing the laws, and making the economic decisions, that affect them most: to perform important guardian functions jointly, in collaboration with fellow citizens, while minimizing reliance on individual guardian roles. Because direct participation, as we've defined it, mandates consensus, decisions arrived at through an iterative process of stakeholder consent would have very low cost of enforcement. That is, because the terms of those decisions would have been developed through serial, popular voting, refined and modified after each round of ballots to accommodate reasonable objections, individual acceptance and commitment to them would be high. In public law, this would result in fewer judicial challenges and secret evasions. In business, it would result in greater personal commitment and organizational effectiveness. It would not be utopia, but it would avoid the dystopias created by centuries of compulsory guardianism.

Most likely, a practical social contract, or constitution, for consensual participation would be based in part on principles drawn from contract law, incorporating such ideas as voluntary entry, reciprocity, affirmative obligations, and the means for auditing performance and enforcing key provisions, resolving disputes, and so on. The first big implication of this is that we could no longer force citizenship and lifelong, compulsory guardianship onto people at birth, but would allow them to voluntarily accept or reject self-governance upon reaching legal age. To people steeped in guardian culture, this will sound like a formula for absolute chaos, but it can be implemented in ways that support public order, and respects civil rights (at all ages), yet harness the power of commitment available only from voluntarism and consent.

For example, minors already possess an abridged set of civil rights: there are many things people who have not yet reached legal age simply cannot do. Under consensual democracy, the only change from current practice would be that, upon reaching the age of emancipation, citizens would have the option of voluntarily accepting the rights and responsibilities of full participation, or remaining (also voluntarily) under some form of guardianship until such time in the future, if ever, that they decide to join the demos. Such a society would be freer, (we currently have no choice about accepting or rejecting guardianship as adults) and those–the vast majority, we might assume–who voluntarily accept the mantle of full citizenship would be much more conscientious about, and committed to, participation.

We can imagine this important life passage taking place as a solemn yet joyous public or private ceremony, perhaps individually (the way military officers and public officials are sworn in) or as a group (the way students graduate from high school and college, or immigrants become naturalized citizens). It could even be done on a cohort basis–say, once a year or once every three years–if the demos thought that was wiser. The point is, such civic ceremonies would mark a significant psychological and political rite of passage and create a specific and legally binding locus of powers within each citizen–a kind of "pledge of allegiance to ourselves" that makes the participative social contract reciprocal among all members of the demos. This "license to self-govern" would last a lifetime, or until renounced by the individual (at which time guardianship would be reimposed) or removed by the state after judicial due process, such as a major felony conviction.

What is the substance of this new voluntary citizenship? First and foremost, it would value and emphasize shared autonomy: individualism within a social setting. It would not abandon hierarchy—as human beings, we are incapable of that—but reject involuntary, coercive hierarchies and the institutions that preserve them. Wherever possible, our systems, procedures, and decisions would encourage heterarchy, or coordination of society's functions by members of co-equal groups, minimizing reliance on centralized and authoritarian command and control by guardians. (Yes, there would still be guardians, if for no other reason than to participate as proxies for those who do not wish to, or cannot, participate themselves; and public officials in the executive branch would still perform many guardian functions—but with oversight and accountability to the demos, not to other guardians—more about that shortly.)

Under heterarchy, citizens would freely choose careers, social and civic roles, place of residence, and marital status, and make consumption and lifestyle choices as they always have. Hierarchies will inevitably form within these voluntary associations, but unlike guardian hierarchies, they would be informal and based on mutual recognition and acceptance of individual merit, accomplishments, and whatever other qualities seemed relevant to the group's stakeholders—including the skills of consensus-building. These are all qualities that would cause others to look to those people voluntarily for leadership and advice. As long as such hierarchies are informal, permit free entry and exit, hold people democratically accountable for what they do, and facilitate the broader functions of participation, they should pose no threat to freedom and fairness.

To make large-scale heterarchy practical, we would cultivate in our children an appetite for genuine consensus, teaching them (and demonstrating ourselves) the skills and patience needed to achieve it. At the same time, we would devalue the hollow, artificial unity generated by unreflective national and group chauvinism—the divide-and-conquer, faction- and empire-building tools of guardians. Instead, we would hold the common good and general will—as established through actual polling and participation—to be our main criteria for regulating society, being constantly alert for would-be guardians who try to plead special interests as common problems and substitute particular preferences for the general will.

Of course, direct participation has practical limits, and it is here that our commitment to self-governance will face its first big test. It's hard to imagine a system of consensual democracy that, even theoretically, allows every citizen to exercise all possible democratic rights in every possible situation and location. Everyone would be so busy minding everyone else's business, as well as their own, that no business at all would get done–a logical absurdity. Instead, we might imagine a more fluid system in which people decide their direct participation is critical in some areas, optional in others, and unnecessary or irrelevant in the remainder.

In the first case, they would register themselves as permanent members of the demos, or set of demos, that affect them most. This is not the bookkeeping nightmare some might imagine. We already do it when we register to vote, pay our taxes, sign up for Social Security, become a shareholder-of-record in a corporation, join a club, receive credit cards or a mortgage, and so on–the processes here would be little different.

In the second case, where their interests were only occasionally involved, they would register themselves as conditional members–perhaps subject to some criteria for active participation when decisions of a certain type are required. Again, this may seem like a logistical nightmare until you consider how many categories of conditional or limited participation already exist: taxpayer (city, county, regional, state, and special assessment districts), member (various clubs and service groups, including home-owner associations), owner (general partner, limited partner, common or preferred stockholder, fee-simple land holder, etc.), lender (from personal loans to bond purchasers), and beneficiary (from a plethora of insurance types to welfare and subsidy recipients of government programs). Where there is a will, there is a way–and more likely than not, a form already exists.

In the third case, although they may follow political and economic events in many areas, they would not be considered members of those demos–although they remain potential members because their life situation, such as job or place of residence, may change. In other words, while we may be stakeholders in principle in all the processes and activities of a consensually democratic society, we are material stakeholders in only a relative few; and it is in those areas that we would exercise our statutory rights to participate.

For example, a typical citizen may feel she is a material stakeholder in virtually all the legislation that affects her neighborhood; in most of the legislation that affects her city; and in some of the legislation that affects her state or region. Because national politics potentially affect everyone, she would attend closely to issues proposed for national ballots, especially those in which she feels the common good or some significant moral principle is at stake. Although she would be registered as a material stakeholder in all these various and overlapping political demos, she would not consider herself a material stakeholder in the affairs of other cities and states unless she had some compelling reason to do so, such as a significant economic or social connection to that area. In fact, we can easily imagine the old distinctions of state and county boundaries eventually giving way to more practical divisions of municipalities and regions based on the distribution of population or on other common denominators, such as similar environmental and employment concerns. Political units of the future may very well depend less on geography than on the topology of human thought and actual economic behavior.

In the private sector, she would be a material stakeholder in the enterprise or organization from which she derives a living, as she would be in any affinity, service, and community groups to which she belongs–although here, too, she would make reasonable distinctions among issues and activities nearer to, or more distant from, her practical and moral concerns; and would participate, or decline to participate, accordingly. We might eventually see these peripheral, "boundary spanning" service and community action groups dwindle, since their mission has traditionally been to address social needs unfulfilled by guardians. As the agenda-setting and decision-making demos expands to include the population as a whole, the priorities and resources of government should become better synchronized with the needs and desires of society, making such organizations–at least their lobbying and social service components–redundant.

In both political and economic spheres, we might imagine technology developed specifically to parse stakeholder information speedily and accurately, so that members of each demos need not be inundated with all information about every issue all the time but could self-select information based on personal needs, interests, and intentions. Such technology and services are already in their infancy on the Internet and in cable broadcasting.

Our typical citizen might also consider herself a material stakeholder in the organizations and institutions she depends upon for important products and services, whether those are delivered through market action or by the government; but again, she would not need, or wish, to be a direct participant in all of their decisions all the time. Three criteria would likely guide any citizen's level of participation in such an open-ended demos: Is the product or service really important to me? Is there a lack of plentiful alternatives? Does the business, organization, or institution have the power to compel my acceptance of their decisions, including price, or dictate the conditions of existence for a significant number of other people? If the answer to these questions is yes, then she might rightly consider herself a material stakeholder and wish to participate in the decisions she feels are most important.

Although the potential for overlapping demos seems infinite, in reality, determining which demos citizens belong to, or want to belong to, in any given instance will generally be a function of their personal "comfort meter." If they feel pressured to accept and live with a decision made by someone else, and if that decision materially affects their quality of life–including their moral comfort zone–they are probably material stakeholders in that area and entitled to direct participation in those decisions. Why? Because unless their views have been aired and an attempt has been made to accommodate them (along with the preferences of other, like-minded people), the decision, by definition, cannot reflect the common good. Unless you consent to a course of action, or have had a reasonable opportunity to have your preferences (and those of like-minded stakeholders) accommodated, the decision cannot reflect the general will.

At this point, guardians and their boosters will only shake their heads and complain that any society operating under such participative rules will be so cumbersome, unproductive, and contentious that nobody would want to live in it. This attitude is perfectly understandable when you consider that their point of reference is the current guardian system in which economic and political elites consider "public input" purely optional. They accept other views only when they are forced upon them—as in periodic elections, consumer boycotts, and adverse legal judgments. Suppose, however, that the people living in, and voluntarily joining, a directly participative system have not been raised in the current coercive, adversarial guardian culture, but have been brought up to value personal agency and reciprocity, and are well-schooled in the arts of consensus-finding—believing passionately that a fair and inclusive democratic process is at least as important as any specific decision, although the content of that decision may be near and dear to their hearts. Under these conditions, it is not only possible to imagine such a society running smoothly and productively (but with less conflict, not more), and with far more resources available for achieving individual, group, community, and national goals than when those resources must be continually annexed, expropriated, hoarded, and defended from angry, anxious competitors.

Of course, freedom from compulsory guardianship implies the freedom to choose guardianship, in one or more areas, if a citizen thinks it is in his or her best interest. After all, life is composed of cycles wherein our emotional and financial resources wax and wane, where our attention is, and ought to be, focused on personal or family affairs; business and career concerns; community service; or intellectual and artistic pursuits. And even an "aristocracy of everyone" cannot legislate more hours to a day. When a balanced life includes a portion of all the things it takes to be human, we must ration our time. Besides, in a democracy, a healthy demos depends mainly on our joint, ongoing, and cumulative contributions, not the heroic performance of a few "super beings"—the old guardian model. Even if governments and companies don't actively facilitate these cycles (sometimes they already do, and we would expect them to do more under consensual democracy), they should at least put no barriers in the way of people trying to cope with the changing patterns of life. In addition to taking periodic leave from our duties to the demos, we may wish to empower specific individuals to act on our behalf—to hold our revocable proxy (perhaps a standardized, simple instrument with an automatic expiration date unless it is renewed) and act as our temporary guardian in one or more areas until we wish to resume those duties ourselves.

Naturally, we can imagine a host of abuses potentially arising from this system—from ambitious would-be guardians snapping up proxies and banking them from disinterested citizens, or citizens pooling them to guarantee support for a particular candidate or initiative—but keep in mind that such "paper empires" can instantly evaporate like morning dew on a given date. And, of course, they would be subject to the same regulations, controls, and audits as other polling methods. The main advantage of such a system is that guardianship, while no longer being imposed on anyone who doesn't want it, would not be denied to those who do.

Along these lines—particularly during the period of transition from representation to participation (especially during the phasing out of the so-called lower houses of legislation, such as the House of Representatives and state assemblies)—it may be wise to retain some kind of upper house as a "constitutional council," restoring the original purpose of such bodies: to give "advice and consent" to the executive branch and basic legislative arm. The main function of this quasi-guardian group would be to review, endorse, or send back for further deliberation and refinement the bills originating from citizen initiatives and the executive branch. This "recycling" of a flawed proposal would not constitute a conventional veto—only a measure's author would have the power to withdraw it. Rather, the council's focus would be on legal form and congruence to a participative constitution when a bill's rejection in judicial review seemed likely. Although the makeup of this body should spark a lively and healthy debate, several potential forms seem most obvious and useful.

One method would be to create a "senate" in the original, Roman sense: a body composed of ex-officials previously elected to the executive branch. This has two advantages. First, it guarantees that members of the upper house would have previous, significant government experience—particularly in living with the day-to-day, administrative effects of laws. Second, it means its members, at one time or another, had been democratically evaluated and endorsed by voters. This ex officio duty could carry a fixed term, the way members of the armed forces leaving active duty are obliged to continue in reserve status for several years. This upper house could also be "virtual" in nature; in the age of e-mail, the Internet, teleconferencing, and whatever communication miracles the future has in store, there is simply no reason for its members to ever meet face to face. This would allow the upper house to become very big indeed, harnessing Condorcet's Rule to make its consensual decisions even wiser. The key thing to remember, though, is that its members would not be guardians in the traditional sense. They could pass no laws binding other people nor could they prevent indefinitely worthy measures from receiving public consideration. They would simply be a rotating panel that assists the demos (of which they are still part) and the executive branch in conducting their lawful business.

Another option would be to fill this advisory council with citizens randomly selected from the broadest possible spectrum of economic and social groups. Because it would statistically reflect the demos, this council could become a forum for special pleading–a place where interest and identity groups, community activists, and others could receive a forum to air their views in parallel with the citizen initiative system, or to "test drive" their ideas before presenting them to the demos. Of course, recommendations of the council, however constituted, could only go forward on a consensual basis, and membership would rotate fairly frequently, so it would not be a return to "politics as usual." However, such a forum would give would-be guardians an outlet for their energies during the period of transition and take a certain amount of pressure off the initiative system.

Along these lines, a corollary institution–but one that is permanent and much more decentralized, numerically larger, and useful in a variety of roles–would be a system of civic jury-commissioners. Even under guardianism, citizens currently provide oversight of certain government activities through such standing agencies as police and fire commissions, public utilities commissions, local school boards, and grand juries. While these institutions currently strive in their own way to bring expertise, common sense, and objectivity to the activities they supervise, they all have one common failing: the people who serve on them want to be commissioners. They eventually view themselves not as citizen-watchdogs but as true-blue guardians–and many, if not most, aspire to higher guardian office. (Grand juries are especially vulnerable to guardian abuse, since many trial rules don't apply at grand jury hearings, and these standing panels often become the pawns of ambitious prosecutors.) While there's nothing wrong with volunteerism that springs from public spirit and a desire to grow as a human being, volunteering to satisfy a need to control others, or to compel people to accept a particular point of view, is the motivation of guardians, not democrats. Even in our current system, service on trial juries excludes volunteers–and for good reason. While citizens may enjoy serving on a jury and can learn a lot from the experience, they may not seek or campaign to join a particular jury, since that brings a personal agenda to what ought to be, and must be, an impartial public duty.

Thus, in a system of consensual democracy, seats on citizen jury-commissions should go not to people who seek them, but to people who, although willing and qualified to serve, don't choose specifically how that service will be realized. Rolls for potential juror-commissioners may be assembled and maintained much as jury lists are kept today or rolls of recruits are kept by selective service boards, with vacancies filled by periodic lotteries. This random factor will alarm many guardians, but random selection does not preclude competence if candidates are drawn from an appropriate stratum. Stratified sampling has long been the norm in marketing and social science research, and already forms the basis for trial jury selection, military draft, tax audits, and many other functions. There is no reason why the pool for a particular jury-commission can't be stratified as to education, age, work experience, and other criteria relevant to a given function, and its members be compensated for a fixed period of service.

The key idea here is that juror-commissioner service should be viewed as a citizen duty, not a career move. It should require some, but not unreasonable, sacrifice. Its main reward will be an opportunity to increase one's democratic learning, improve one's personal skills and network of acquaintances, and serve the community—doing one's part to keep the democratic system safe, just as soldiers make sacrifices to defend the nation from aggressors. If the jury-commission system is implemented step-by-step, concurrent with the democratization of education and other social and political institutions, it should produce results no worse than our current system of patronage and careerism, and probably a good deal better.

In short, to a mature and educated democrat, direct participation is not an invitation to micromanage the world, only to play a measured part in determining the common good and achieving the general will. What may seem on the surface to be a hopelessly complex web of interconnected and conflicting interests is, in reality, just a snapshot of how human lives are already being lived. When all our snapshots are assembled into a grand mosaic—a portrait of the demos—it is obvious that some individual tendrils extend more deeply than others into some parts of society. It is the right and prerogative of citizen-workers to decide which of these roots anchor and nourish their lives best at any given time, then act accordingly. It means, as Robert Bellah puts it, "a reapportion of the idea of vocation or calling, a return in a new way to the idea of work as a contribution to the good of all and not merely as a means to one's own advancement."[124]

In politics, it should be no more difficult for an individual citizen to enter the "political market"–say, as a candidate for executive office, or with a ballot initiative–than it is to enter an economic market with a new product or service. That is, the degree of difficulty should be proportional to the level of office or size of the demos affected: neighborhood issues and local offices being the easiest; national issues and offices being the toughest. Agenda-setting and decision-making at all these levels should be open to all members of a particular demos who are willing to put in the time and effort to participate meaningfully. Also like the development of a new product, getting items on the demos's agenda should involve some practical hurdles. It is to everyone's best interest to allow thoughtful, necessary, useful, and innovative proposals to move forward while giving impulsive, half-baked, or anti-democratic proposals opportunities for second thoughts, cooling off, and (if still desired) reformulation.

These checkpoints needn't be too stringent or arbitrary. Rather, they should be based on a reasonable combination of publicly available guidelines plus peer (citizen-jury or constitutional council) review that would either advance a proposal or send it back for further work–decisions that, in case of deadlock or intransigence, could be overturned by gathering more signatures or appealing to the judiciary. However, if the rules governing citizen proposals are themselves developed consensually, the procedure won't be too onerous. We may take comfort in the knowledge that many, if not most, crackpot and oppressive proposals in the past originated in response to guardian actions or the fear of potential guardian actions. With the threat of non-consensual coercive laws reduced, motivation for extreme proposals will be reduced as well.

Information gathering, personal deliberation, and iterative voting–all aimed at approaching consensus–should be promoted by stewards of the process (government and corporate officials) and should be as easy and straightforward as possible. Some have already proposed that each citizen be given a secure e-mail address to conduct democratic business, including communication with other citizens as well as with state officials–and

---

124 Bellah. *Habits of the Heart.* 287.

who knows what better systems future technology may bring.[125] For example, Internet expert Steven Johnson foresees decentralized systems that use ideologically neutral filters, screens, and statistical processing to make available to users information about not only the suggestions and preferences of fellow citizens, but the ranking and distribution of reactions to those views, flagging but not marginalizing controversial (and possibly very innovative and useful) new ideas.[126]

No matter what system is used, however, government and private-sector facilitators must maintain these facilities and rights-related records as scrupulously as they currently maintain social security, tax, and financial accounting information–a tall task, but not an impossible one. Citizen access to the system for purposes of participation, verification, and audit must not be unduly limited or expensive. Such a system would not be cheap, but the human and financial resources wasted over centuries of guardian exploitation and folly have been vastly greater. If a democratic nation can justify lavish spending on anything, it is on the process that keeps them free.

One early, time-consuming but essential task for new citizen-legislators would be to systematically review, renew, modify, or repeal centuries' worth of guardian law that had been thrust upon us without democratic consent. This process would not be as daunting and destabilizing as some might think. Even under guardianship, old laws are regularly revisited, amended, and repealed; and many states have "sunset law" provisions wherein a statute expires after a given term unless it is specifically renewed. In any case, there is no reason to think that good laws won't survive consensual citizen review, and that the worst laws won't perish, as they should. Those that remain would be stripped of their guardian bias and fortified, as appropriate, with democratic values and procedures. This will be an

---

125 Aversa, Jeannine. Associated Press. "Give Everyone an E-mail Address, Report Says," *San Francisco Chronicle*, November 22, 1995; FM-2030 "Our Political Process Suits the 18th Century," *Los Angeles Times*, May 15, 1992; Katch, M. Ethan. *The Electronic Media and the Transformation of Law*. Oxford: Oxford University Press. 1991; Morris, Regan. Associated Press. "Singapore Ruled by E-Government," *San Francisco Chronicle*, December 12, 2000; "Dell enters electronic voting venture," (AP), *San Francisco Chronicle*, June 5, 2001.

126 Johnson. *Emergence*. 161.

enormous effort–probably taking decades–but it need be done only once. Future generations will not feel burdened by the laws they inherit because that inheritance will include a consensual means for modifying or repealing those rules that no longer work.

Another early and recurring task will be for citizen-legislators to devise and approve an equitable tax policy and allocate public funds to major budget categories. While detailed budget administration will always be a job for the executive branch, allocation of tax money into general budget categories–from defense and public works to welfare–should be made by the demos itself. This power is crucial if democratic choices are to have any meaning, popular control over the bureaucracy is to have any teeth, and democratic learning is to have any depth. Every law has its consequences, including economic costs and other side effects, such as unforseen conflicts with other statutes. Rules for citizen initiatives, guidelines from elected executives, and advice from government agencies (including specialized juror-commissions and a constitutional council) can all help make sure that new laws stay aligned with current allocations, or can trigger new allocations and increased funding, including new taxation or debt financing, when they do not.

One key ingredient–perhaps the most important single element–to this consensual process is abandoning the one-time, win-lose, majority-rule voting system so beloved by adversarial guardians. Serial voting (that is, voting several times on the same issue over weeks or months so that each voter can learn what other voters think, and sponsors can upgrade their proposals as they learn about voter preferences) and multiple-choice ballots (presenting complex issues in a more realistic way than as simple, binary choices) offer one approach to large-scale consensus-building. Each successive vote on major issues would see its authors modify the proposition, a little or a lot, to accommodate minority positions. Eventually, differences in opinions and preferences would narrow until something approaching the general will is established. This form of consensus-building is not perfect, and the demos would have to agree ahead of time on what sort of final majority or number of iterations constitutes an operational consensus. (Since it is not a one-time, win-lose vote, and since the basic proposition will be modified during the serial polling process, the supermajority problem should not arise.) However, even if the final, very small opposing minority still objects to the law, they cannot claim that it was passed unfairly, or impulsively, or with the undue influence of special interests, or at the pleasure of a few guardians, or that every procedural effort was not made to accommodate their views. After all, the goal of a new, consensual democratic social contract is not to eliminate all coercion in government; only to minimize it and ensure that, when coercion is necessary, it will have the moral force of the general will behind it.

Another important area for citizen-legislator oversight is war powers. Too often, guardians use military action, or the threat of war, as a way to suppress dissent or rally support for a troubled administration. Also, armed conflict gives guardians a chance to demonstrate their leadership in dramatic circumstances and "earn their place in history"–a temptation that will continue for chief executives under consensual democracy. To counteract these pressures, Jean Bethke Elshtain counsels a return to the model of the "chastened patriot," giving war powers to citizens who have "no illusions" and recognize "the limiting conditions internal to international politics...." These "civic beings" would "...not embrace utopian fantasies or world government or total disarmament,"[127] but would represent a repository of common sense and moral gravity formed when the people who work and pay taxes, raise children, fight and die as soldiers, or suffer as civilians make the ultimate decisions about war and peace. There is compelling evidence that the more democratic a nation becomes, the less inclined it is to wage war with its neighbors,[128] a cause for optimism in a world that is already turning its back on autocrats and oligarches.

There is no question that security for the demos, even in peacetime, requires armed forces that can respond quickly to emergencies. There is no question, too, that the more those armed forces resemble the demos, both in composition and ambitions, the safer the state and its democratic practices will be from military usurpation. Thus, the government's chief executive, while serving at the pleasure of the demos and commanding the state's military, should be prohibited from authorizing acts of war under any conditions other than immediate national threat, unless specifically

---

127 Elshtain, Jean Bethke. *Women and War*. New York: Basic Books. 1987.
128 Weart, Spencer R. *Never at War: Why Democracies Will Not Fight One Another*. New Haven: Yale University Press.

authorized by the demos, or at least the constitutional council. Even then, such acts must be subject to early review, and the decision to continue a war, as well as start one, should be left to the people who will bear its burdens.

In property law, consensual participation means reviving the Enlightenment idea that a corporation is a construct of the state, created to serve the public interest. Corporate social and democratic responsibilities, therefore, would not be options left to the preferences of economic guardians but would be an integral part of the corporate charter, shaped and guided by its material stakeholders. Employees would be defined not just as limited agents of the corporation, subject to (or exempted from) certain labor regulations, health codes, and so on, but a locus of democratic rights–just as customers "purchase" certain democratic rights when they buy and depend upon a product or service.

From this perspective, proprietorships, partnerships, and closely held corporations would behave more like publicly held companies, since their material stakeholders must have the opportunity to participate in decisions that were previously monopolized by owners and financiers. Bellah and Dewey, among others, view democratizing such entities as key not only to improving individual lives, but to creating a true life of the community: "It is a widely held middle-class–and American–view that through work one gains self-respect and the ability to control, at least in part, one's environment. In this understanding, compassion takes the form of 'helping others to help themselves.'"[129]

In the private sector, the trend toward consensual task- and oversight-groups that mix guardians and workers is already well established. It would be a relatively short step to constitute these groups more democratically, without resorting to representation (although that may be a necessary, transitional step), and to give these groups real power to make binding, as well as advisory, decisions once property laws have been updated.

Chief among these legal reforms would be democratizing the rules concerning boards of directors, now filled mainly with a company's top executives, colleague guardians from other firms, and a few token directors from vocal interest groups, such as unions and social activists. Instead

---

129 Bellah. *Habits of the Heart.* 287.

of choosing them by a vote confined to shareholders (usually, endorsement of a fixed slate proposed by current directors, with no competition–a plutocracy in which each share, not each person, counts as one vote), the board would be elected by all material stakeholders, from a pool of all material stakeholders, and perform the function of an upper house as the firm's "constitutional council," advising and facilitating the directly participative management of the company's operational units.

Chief among these democratically controlled operational and planning decisions would be those involving the company's resource allocations: the acquisition and use of capital and the disposition of any surpluses generated by market action. While such allocations and distributions may wind up essentially the same as under guardianism, participation by material stakeholders will vastly increase their perceived fairness and society's confidence that economic justice has been done, reducing the threat of public outcry and intervention by the state. Only consensual democracy offers the possibility of distributing wealth unequally but justly–in accordance with the widest possible perception of fairness, especially when that perception changes over time.

However, we can assume that in many enterprises, democratic allocations and distributions may differ substantially from guardian patterns, especially when legal constraints favoring guardians have been removed. For example, stakeholders may prefer that profits be put into a sinking fund (essentially, a revolving debit account) which may be drawn down for any consensual purpose, such as funding new ventures. For individuals, some system of microloans may prove popular and become a substantial substitute for public relief. For real property, proportional ownership would be defined by material stakeholders: those with significant interests in financing and using the property. Lenders would remain material stakeholders, but their rights would be more as limited partners than as proprietors–foreclosure would generally not be an option since it preempts, and does not promote, collaborative and consensual solutions. A primary residence purchased through debt or occupied by rents would be viewed first and foremost as a locus of democratic sovereignty, and only secondarily as a commodity. Anyone living in a dwelling would be a material stakeholder in its democratic management, and rights of citizenship would prevail over any competing rights of property–although, if consensual decision-making is observed, these conflicts should be few and none should prove intractable. That percentage of rents constituting economic surplus would accumulate in a portable equity account, which accrues to material stakeholders (including tenants, no matter how many times they move). This account is a tangible claim against the real estate they defend as citizens, and it becomes a source of wealth that may be drawn upon in time of need, or for any other use. To encourage new housing development, we might initially treat rental property like copyrighted material: that is, the developer and financiers could have a temporary monopoly on these benefits, including surplus (as they do now), but only for a fixed and limited period.

These are just a few ideas for broadening the basis of property ownership and reconciling current differences between domain and dominion. Certainly other, better ideas will follow once the resources of the entire demos begin to address the problem.

Of course, committed guardians will immediately object to this scheme, claiming it would create a bookkeeping nightmare; but remember, similar accounts are already in place, from social security and income tax to credit-card balances and even an airline's frequent-flyer miles–trivial pursuits compared to the grave issue of domain versus dominion. Besides, "community property" has long been used as a legal fiction for preserving equity in marriages between partners of unequal economic strength. As Harvard's Joint Center for Housing Studies, interpreting Census Bureau statistics, concluded, current guardian-biased property laws contribute to, "...some of the worst social problems facing the nation, among them slums, discrimination, drugs, unemployment, crime and political instability."[130] It is hard to imagine a social problem more in need of, and more amenable to, democratic solutions.

To participate in all of this, material stakeholders needn't be paragons of virtue. All they really need do is distinguish their own long- versus short-term interests, because the further we look into the future, the more obvious it becomes that our social cooperation is essential–a form of enlightened self-interest. We'll need no corporate or political guardians

---

130 Cunniff, John. Associated Press. "Home ownership may be key to solving social problems," *San Francisco Examiner*, March 19, 1995.

to compel us to make sacrifices for the common good because we, voluntarily and separately as well as jointly, recognize what is essential to our long-term interests. At this stage of enlightenment, we need no longer pass laws enforcing our own version of the work ethic onto welfare recipients, for example, or force assimilation (or conversely, group isolation), onto new immigrants—these issues will take care of themselves through the open-ended agenda-setting and consensus-finding process of direct participation. All we really need do is to imagine the kind of society we each want to inhabit, and want our children to inhabit, and consistently bias our individual decisions in that direction. Through inclusive, democratic practices in both politics and economics, these individual visions will gradually become shared visions. This shared vision, even with the wide variations inevitable in a large demos, will become our first great consensus: that direct democracy is the best possible long-term investment in ourselves.

How might the shift away from guardianism toward full citizen participation begin? What would life in a direct democracy be like, particularly during the all-important decades of transition?

We shouldn't expect conflict to disappear simply because we've reached a consensus that guardianism is harmful and participation is good. In truth, the level of conflict in daily life will undoubtedly increase during our rather extended period of transition from dependency to shared autonomy—mostly because we will no longer have, or feel comfortable about appealing to, parent-guardians for help. We *can* expect our resolutions to those conflicts to be more effective and last longer than they do today; they will not devolve, as they have in the past, into cyclic power struggles where today's smug, ambitious winners become tomorrow's bitter, vengeful losers.

Problems will arise where we least expect them. For example, judicial review—originally conceived as a way to keep one branch of government from poaching on another or breaching the constitution—has had just the opposite effect under guardianism. Knowing there are no real penalties for encroachment, guardians wishing to expand their power regularly push their decisions past the limits, relying on activist judges to back them up. We may infer from this that as long as guardian-arbiters are available, ambitious advocates will use them to avoid consensus. One way to minimize this risk is to mandate democratic consensus-finding within the judicial branch as well as the legislative and executive; to limit the ability of any one judge, or small panel of judges, to overturn with ease a decision arrived at through the incremental, consensus-building process.

We might also anticipate problems with people who make a fetish of "original intent." Thomas Jefferson famously suggested that all laws, including constitutions, should expire every twenty years, forcing each generation to think for itself. By now, it should be apparent that the U.S. Constitution has been re-worked so often over the years—not just by amendments, but by judicial activists stretching the boundaries of the law—that original intent can be used to defend almost any position. What "original intent-ers" overlook is that, where the Constitution is strong—where it has survived with its initial form in tact—is where it deals with process. Where it is weak, and where it has been subject to continual, torturous reinterpretation and abuse, is where it deals with content: what we are supposed to do as opposed to how we should go about it. A new or modified, more directly participative constitution—and the people who use it—would do well to keep this in mind.

Repression by guardians who see their power waning will be another major obstacle to launching consensual democracy. Even the most blood-less and benign "revolution" invites counterrevolution by those who feel they have the most to lose. The real risk to a new, more democratic social contract is not that self-governing citizens will ruin civilization, but that the last generation of guardians will use their remaining powers to repress them—to represent their personal emergency as a public disaster. During times of crisis and uncertainty, attractive and persuasive guardians will always step forward and claim to have a solution. The price of obtaining it will be what it has always been: the freedom of the demos.

In the economic sphere, last-gasp guardian reaction may take the form of an intense and prolonged "capital strike": intentional misallocation or withholding of investments, compensation, capital goods, and other resources from consensually defined uses as a means of punishing partici-pants and re-exerting guardian control—as least as long as old laws regard-ing non-democratic property rights still permit it. Such action needn't be conspiratorial, formal, or even well-organized to have effect; and dem-ocratic-minded citizens may find themselves hard-pressed to keep their reforms on track when the economic outlook seems bleak; or, even more dangerously, to resist the urge of abandoning reform and adopting guardian tactics themselves.

Fortunately, the threat of a serious capital strike imperiling a nation like the United States is remote. For one thing, America is just too big a marketplace to be ignored for long. The temptation for some guardians to break ranks and resume productive activity will be too strong, especially if the bottom line really is their chief concern: nothing about democratic governance says a firm must be unprofitable. Although economic guardians will lose their monopoly over resources and the use of surplus, they will still have say in the process. After a suitable show of outrage, punctuated no doubt by lengthy lawsuits, we might expect these clever and acquisitive minds to go back to doing what they do best: figuring new angles for wringing profit and power out of whatever the system has to offer. Besides, in the last analysis, sovereignty is trumps. Economic guardians can do only what the law allows, or else they become outlaws–and going to jail is bad for business.

Many people–ordinary citizens not just guardians–will also complain that consensual democracy, with its frequent, serial, multiple-choice ballots and all the requisite controls, communications, and information services in place, is just too time-consuming and expensive, as is the process of citizen initiatives. They will advocate expediency over procedure and ignore the long history of hidden costs that is the legacy of guardianism: human and monetary costs which, over the centuries, dwarf those of even the most ambitious participative systems. After a rather confusing and unsettling period of transition, though, government under consensual democracy will unquestionably be cheaper because, with the rules of political economy based mostly on consensus, fewer laws (and legal loopholes) will exist, the cost of enforcement will be lower, and the wasteful flip-flops of policies and programs endemic to competitive guardianism will be a thing of the past. This, perhaps, is consensual democracy's most wonderful paradox: the larger it gets, the smaller the machinery of state coercion needs to be.

The relationship between the demos and mass media will also change under consensual democracy. Right now, print and broadcast policies are based on long-established rights of property: they are empowered by law to promote the media owners' view,[131] or to sell as many papers (or as much advertising) as possible, which often means pandering to the sensational and accentuating the negative—things that appeal most to a disengaged and cynical mass audience. However, as the number of guardians dwindle, the owners of mass media will have fewer guardian allies to promote or guardian enemies to pillory, and the value of their partisan "editorial product" will diminish. Further, as more guardian functions are undertaken by rotating juror-commissioners and by the demos itself, the news will likely become more issue-driven and less focused on sensation and celebrity. Although top elective, executive-branch offices and senior bureaucratic positions will always attract natural guardians, the more these offices are viewed as noble and necessary—but unglamorous—positions whose powers are circumscribed by the democratic process, the fewer Napoleons and Caesars will seek them. The commercial mass media will always have a role in entertainment, information, and advocacy. But as its policies are increasingly set by stakeholder consensus and its monopoly on mass communications undercut by the Internet and other future, citizen-to-citizen technologies, its power to act irresponsibly or capriciously will be limited.

James Madison proclaimed that a sovereign people has a right to make a constitution on "great extraordinary occasions." Legal historian Bruce Ackerman, surveying America's civil upheavals, offers a rule of thumb for recognizing when such conditions exist.[132] In order to justify altering a fundamental basis for government, he says, some 20 percent of citizens must give the proposed change "deep support." That is, they must have given it at least as much thought as they would to any major life decision, such as getting married, changing a career, having a child, or submitting to a risky medical procedure. Additionally, another 31 percent—citizens who are less politically aware, but are responsible people who look to opinion leaders for their cues—must agree that change is needed. This provides a bare majority, enough to gain the attention of guardians and pollsters. If discontent is sufficient and a better alternative seems feasible, this major-

---

131 Associated Press. "4 in 10 Journalists Soften, Avoid Stories Due to Pressure," *San Francisco Chronicle*, May 1, 2000.

132 Ackerman, Bruce. *We the People: Vol. I, Foundations.* Cambridge; Harvard University Press. 1992.

ity can serve as a critical mass upon which consensus for change is built. Certainly, if such percentages are ever approached, they would represent a vastly greater number of people, even as a fraction of the population, than the number of Americans who ratified the first constitution or supported the Revolutionary War.

Like most major life changes, the transition to consensual democracy is best made in incremental steps. Participative democrats are, after all, mature citizens: evolutionaries, not revolutionaries. They do not recognize their need and capacity for self-governance overnight. They do not expect to remake in six Biblical days a culture that took millennia to create. However, incremental steps do not preclude milestones. Here are some that might serve as significant waypoints on this path to a better future.

Advocates of direct participation–Cronin, Barber, and others–have made practical proposals for establishing a national initiative system which, given the general trend toward more democratic institutions and the strong social contract that has arisen between citizens and the federal state, now seems inevitable to even the staunchest guardians.[133] Most of these are modeled on successful state systems, and all operate in parallel with the existing congressional system. Whichever is adopted, it will be our college for large-scale democratic learning, just as state systems have been our nursery. However, this will not be the end of our democratic education or our experiments in self-government, only the beginning.

When it comes to deeper levels of participation, it is likely that guardians in one state, or states in a region known for strong individualist traditions such as the Northeast or Rocky Mountain West, will trust their citizens enough to make a substantial shift toward large-scale democracy in economic institutions and at other levels in government. These pilot experiments will require enabling laws (not the least of which is a waiver of Article IV, Section 4, of the U.S. Constitution, which requires all states to be republics), including corresponding amendments to each state's constitution. The vehicle for change here would not be the usual organs of representation–laws passed by legislatures with diminishing powers–but a coherent structure of amendments and laws, passed through initiatives,

---

133 Broder, David S. *Democracy Derailed: Initiative Campaigns and the Power of Money.* New York: A James H. Silberman Book/Harcourt. 2000.

that would take effect over time, perhaps even decades, giving stakeholders plenty of time to anticipate new procedures, simulate their workings, and iron out as many bugs as possible before they begin to use them.

At the national level, such changes must eventually be codified in a new or revised constitution. This could be done through the traditional amendment process, but this procedure gives most power to state and congressional guardians–the very people most likely to view such changes as dire personal threats. Even worse, constitutions forged and implemented by existing governments (that is, constitutional convention representatives who go on to rule in its name) have not fared well. Such constitutions lose value as social contracts and are quickly viewed as mere guardian legislation, subject to frequent appeals and modification. Thus, the sovereign demos itself, using sequential, consensual methods, is a much better custodian of this framing process and its ratification. To ensure social and economic stability during this period, it seems wise to view the new constitution as an extension of the old one and to continue certain guardian roles during this time. After ratification, the basic unit of democracy would shift from guardians to individual citizens. For the first time in our history, we would truly be a government of, by, and for the people.

Let nobody doubt it: shifting from guardianism to self-governance will open a Pandora's Box. It will bring forth both anticipated and unforeseeable problems as well as a wealth of new energy and benefits–more profound than our shift from monarchy to republic. We will have tasted forbidden fruit, become aware of our political nakedness, and found shame in our status as dependents. When we realize that such knowledge has expelled us forever from our previous fool's paradise, the serious and joyful task of building a truly self-governing society can begin.

While most people will flourish as collaborative, self-directing democrats, some will not; and establishing a thoroughly just and prosperous society through our own efforts will be as difficult as the process of growing up. History shows that the people who do best during times of turmoil often do poorly when things return to normal: when ambiguity gives way to certainty, patience and compassion replace ambition and agitation, and due process, not heroic improvisation, becomes the norm. No less a pragmatic visionary than John Maynard Keynes reminds us that "... the task of transmuting human nature must not be confused with the task of managing it."[134] Russian radical Alexander Herzen wrote in the mid-1800s that a new form of human sacrifice had arisen in his time: the proffering of human beings on the altars of abstraction and slaughtering them wholesale in the name of nation, church, party, class, progress, or to summon an inevitable future. Our instincts, alas, haven't changed much since his day. Isaiah Berlin warned that a society's first public obligation is to avoid extremes of suffering—wars, revolutions, assassinations, and pogroms of various kinds—and that remains good advice. A decent society, one based on moral behavior including economic justice and consensus, must not violate other, deeply held and equally important convictions, such as our right to live (or even to seriously mislead) our lives in peace. If this caveat disappoints rabid democrats who may be anxious, once again, to "refresh the tree of liberty with the blood of tyrants," then I am sorry; but as Einstein promised, "There is no a priori reason for believing that the truth, when it is discovered, will necessarily prove interesting"—or exciting, or glorious—or will be consistent with the ambitions or teachings of great guardians from the past.

Our political economy—the sea in which we swim as social animals—is the base matter from which we have fashioned all our golden ages. Our self-direction is the spark that ignites the flame of our nobler instincts and lets them shine. The ultimate guardian argument against popular government is that citizens should not be encouraged to think too much about which laws they'll obey. For guardians, no law or tradition is so sacrosanct that it can't be changed or ignored once "our own people" rise to power. As a result, we have inherited a vast patchwork of laws and customs that are both essential and superfluous, valid and invalid, useful and wasteful. Some enjoy a high degree of consensus—like our laws against abusing children. Others, like the antique "blue laws" of a bygone puritan past, are observed by practically no one. They are the whirlpools, backwaters, and riptides of our communal sea. If we citizens ever claim our natural right to rule ourselves, then the guardian leviathan will sink back into its depths, joining other half-forgotten Western myths—cautionary tales of older, more savage times when giants ruled the earth.

---

134 Keynes, John Maynard. *The General Theory of Employment, Interest, and Money.* London: Macmillan. 1936. 374.

Such a vision is neither conservative nor liberal... It does not seek to return to the harmony of a "traditional" society, though it is open to learning from the wisdom of such societies. ...it insists... that human life is lived in the balance between faith and doubt. Such a vision arises not only from the theories of intellectuals, but from the practices of life that Americans are already engaged in. ... Above all, such a vision seeks the confirmation or correction of discussion and experiment with our friends, our fellow citizens.[135]

---

135 Bellah. *Habits of the Heart.* 296.

BIBLIOGRAPHY AND FURTHER READING

Abramson, Jeffrey. *We, the Jury: The Jury System and the Ideal of Democracy.* New York: Basic Books. 1994.

Ackerman, Bruce. *We the People: Vol. I, Foundations.* Cambridge, Mass.: Harvard University Press. 1992.

Adler, Stephen J. *The Jury: Trial and Error in the American Courtroom.* New York: Doubleday/Main Street. 1995.

Alcaly, Roger E. "Reinventing the Corporation." *New York Review of Books.* April 10, 1997.

Asimov, Nanette. "There's Big Power In the Boycott." *San Francisco Chronicle.* October 2, 1990.

---. "School Board Chief Lags in Child Support: SF official, a parental responsibility advocate, owes $5,000." *San Francisco Chronicle.* May 12, 1997.

Associated Press. "Celebrating the Bill of Rights: Hundreds Queue Up on Bicentennial to Sign and Reaffirm It." *San Francisco Chronicle.* December 16, 1991.

---. "80% in Survey Found Jury Duty to Be an Uplifting Experience." *San Francisco Chronicle.* August 14, 2000.

---. "4 in 10 Journalists Soften, Avoid Stories Due to Pressure." *San Francisco Chronicle.* May 1, 2000.

---. "House GOP Official Admits a Mistake: He handed our PAC checks on the floor," *San Francisco Chronicle.* May 11, 1997.

--- . "LBJ's Doubts About Running: He didn't see himself as best choice in '64, tape shows." *San Francisco Chronicle.* July 19, 1997.

---. "Microloans Help State Business." *San Francisco Chronicle*. Aug. 15, 2000.

---. "Politicians Say Public is Partly to Blame: Anonymous replies to criticism that Congress is ineffective, out of touch, cowardly." *San Francisco Chronicle*. April 6, 1992.

Aversa, Jeannine. Associated Press. "Give Everyone an E-Mail Address, Report Says." *San Francisco Chronicle*. November 22, 1995.

Bailyn, Bernard. Ed. *The Debate on the Constitution, Part 1*. New York: The Library of America. 1993.

--- . *The Debate on the Constitution, Part 2*. New York: The Library of America. 1993.

Barabak, Mark Z. "State Voters Like Initiative Process." *San Francisco Chronicle*. March 10, 1993.

Barber, Benjamin R. *An Aristocracy of Everyone: The Politics of Education and the Future of America*. New York: Oxford University Press. 1992.

--- . *Conquest of Politics: Liberal Philosophy in Democratic Times*. Princeton, N.J.: Princeton University Press. 1988.

Bellah, Robert, et. al. *Habits of the Heart*. Berkeley: University of California Press. 1985.

Berger, Peter L. *The Capitalist Revolution: Fifty Propositions about Prosperity, Equality and Liberty*. New York: Basic Books. 1986.

Berlin, Isaiah. "On the Pursuit of the Ideal." *The New York Review of Books*. March 17, 1988.

--- . *The Sense of Reality: Studies in Ideas and Their History*. Edited by Henry Hardy. New York: Farrar, Straus & Giroux. 1996.

Berthelsen, Christian. "Genesis of State's Energy Fiasco." *San Francisco Chronicle*. December 11, 2000.

Bowles, Samuel, and Gintis, Herbert. *Democracy & Capitalism: Property, Community, and the Contradictions of Modern Social Thought*. New York: Basic Books. 1986.

Broder, David S. *Democracy Derailed: Initiative Campaigns and the Power of Money*. New York: A James H. Silberman Book/Harcourt. 2000.

Bromwich, David. *Politics by Other Means: Higher Education and Group Thinking*. New Haven: Yale University Press. 1992.

Burns, James MacGregor, with Overby, L. Marvin. *Cobblestone Leadership: Majority Rule, Minority Power*. Oklahoma City: University of Oklahoma Press. 1990.

Calvert, Karin. *Children in the House: The Material Culture of Early Childhood, 1600-1900*. Boston: Northeastern University Press. 1994.

Caplin, Andrew, et. al. *Housing Partnerships: A New Approach to a Market at a Crossroads*. Cambridge, Mass.: The MIT Press. 1997.

Chomsky, Noam. *Deterring Democracy*. New York: Hill and Wang. 1991.

(Chronicle Washington Bureau). "Davis Wants His Judges to Stay in Line. *San Francisco Chronicle*. March 1, 2000.

Cloninger, C. Robert. "A Systematic Method for Clinical Description and Classification of Personality Variants." *Archives of General Psychiatry* 44. 1987.

Cohen, Sharon. Associated Press. "Workers Happy to Be in Charge." *San Francisco Chronicle*. December 2, 1990.

Coile, Zachary and Berthelsen, Christian. "Criminal investigation of Enron: Justice Dept. wants to know if energy giant fleeced investors, workers," *San Francisco Chronicle*, January 10, 2002.

Cronin, Thomas E. *Direct Democracy: The Politics of Initiative, Referendum, and Recall*. Cambridge, Mass.: Harvard University Press. 1989.

Cunniff, John. Associated Press. "Home ownership may be key to solving social problems." *The San Francisco Examiner.* March 19, 1995.

Dahl, Robert A. "The Problem of Civic Competence. *Journal of Democracy.* Vol. 3, No. 4. October, 1992.

--- . *A Preface to Economic Democracy.* Berkeley: University of California Press. 1985.

--- . *Democracy and Its Critics*. New Haven: Yale University Press. 1989.

Dahrendorf, Ralf. *The Modern Social Conflict: An Essay on the Politics of Liberty*. New York: Weidenfeld & Nicolson. 1988.

Darwin, Charles. *The Descent of Man, and Selection in the Relation to Sex.* Princeton, N.J.: Princeton University Press. [1871] 1981.

Davis, David Brion. *Revolutions: Reflections on American Equality and Foreign Liberations*. Cambridge, Mass.: Harvard University Press. 1990.

De Vany, Arthur. "In an On-Line Salon, Scientists Sit Back and Ponder 'What Is the Question You Are Asking Yourself?'" *New York Times.* December 30, 1997.

Dewey, John. *Democracy and Education.* New York: The Free Press. 1916.

Dobbyn, Tim. (Reuters). "Airline Competition Has Declined, Panel Told." *San Francisco Chronicle.* March 6, 1998.

Drucker, Peter F. *The New Realities: In Government and Politics/In Economics and Business/In Society and World View*. New York: Harper & Row. 1994.

Dumont, Louis. *Homo Hierarchius: An Essay on the Caste System*. Trans. by Mark Sainsbury. Chicago: University of Chicago Press. 1970.

Dunn, Judy and Munn, Penny. "Becoming a Family Member." *Child Development*. 56. 1985.

Dworkin, Ronald. *Freedom's Law: The Moral Reading of the American Constitution*. Cambridge, Mass.: Harvard University Press. 1996.

--- . *Law's Empire*. Cambridge: Harvard University Press. 1987.

Ehrenhalt, Alan. *The United States of Ambition: Politicians, Power, and the Pursuit of Office*. New York: Times Books/Random House. 1991.

Eliot, Lise. *What's Going On In There? How the Brain and Mind Develop In the First Five Years of Life*. New York: Bantam Books. 1999.

Elshtain, Jean Bethe. *Woman and War*. New York: Basic Books. 1987.

The Federalist. Number 63. 1788.

FM-2030. "Our Political Process Suits the 18th Century." *Los Angeles Times*. May 15, 1992.

Fortune, October 31, 1994.

Fraser, Andrew (Associated Press). "Firms Act as Investor, Lender: Critics say hedge fund bailout smacks of conflict of interests." *San Francisco Chronicle*. October 7, 1998.

Fukuyama, Francis. *Trust: The Social Virtues and the Creation of Prosperity*. New York: The Free Press. 1995.

Gaylin, Willard, MD. *Rediscovering Love.* New York: Viking. 1986.

Geewax, Marilyn. Cox News Service. "The Rich to the Rest of the Us: Let Them Eat Pink Slips." *San Franciso Chronicle.* October 10, 1991.

Gellerman, Saul W. *Motivation and Productivity.* Thirteenth Edition. New York: American Management Association. 1963.

Ginsberg, Benjamin. *The Captive Public: How Mass Opinion Promotes State Power.* New York: Basic Books. 1986.

Glass, James M. *Psychosis and Power: Threats to Democracy in the Self and in the Group.* Ithaca N.Y.: Cornell University Press. 1995.

Gledhill, Lynda. "Ballot Initiatives Trusted More Than Politicians. *San Francisco Chronicle.* November 11, 1999.

Goode, Erica (New York Times). "Incompetent People Really Have No Clue, Studies Find." *San Francisco Chronicle.* January 18, 2000.

Gould, Carol C. *Rethinking Democracy: Freedom and Social Cooperation in Politics, Economy, and Society.* Cambridge, U.K.: Cambridge University Press. 1988.

Grant, Linda. *Los Angeles Times.* "Firms' Futures Rest on More Worker Involvement." *San Francisco Chronicle.* May 4, 1992.

Grossman, Lawrence K. *The Electronic Republic: Reshaping Democracy in the Information Age.* New York: Viking. 1995.

Gruley, Bryan. Gannett News Service. "Executive Pay and Performance: It Doesn't Add Up." *Marin Independent Journal.* November 16, 1991.

Habermas, Jurgen. *Between Facts and Norms: Contributions to A Discourse Theory of Law and Democracy.* Cambridge, Mass.: The MIT Press. 1996.

--- . *Theory and Practice.* Boston: Beacon Press. 1973.

Hamilton, Alexander, Madison, James, and Jay, John. *The Federalist: Or the New Constitution.* New York: The Heritage Press. [1787-88]. 1945.

Harrington, Michael. *Socialism Past and Future.* New York: Arcade. 1989.

Havens, George R. *Voltaire's Marginalia on the Pages of Rousseau.* Ohio: Burt Franklin. 1933.

Heilbroner, Robert L. *Behind the Veil of Economics: Essays in the Worldly Philosophy.* New York: W.W.Norton & Company. 1988.

--- . *The Nature and Logic of Capitalism.* New York: W.W.Norton & Co. 1985.

Hobbes, Thomas. *Leviathan.* Indianapolis: The Bobbs-Merrill Company. 1958.

Hobhouse, Henry. *Forces of Change: An Unorthodox View of History.* Arcade Publishers. 1990.

Hobson, J. Allen, MD. *The Chemistry of Conscious States.* Boston: Little, Brown. 1994.

Hochschild, Adam. "Jurors Weigh the Facts." *San Francisco Chronicle.* July 12, 1988.

Holldobler, Bert, and Wilson, E.O. *The Ants.* Cambridge, Mass.: Harvard University Press. 1990.

Howe, Kenneth. "Big Money Swamps the Ballot: Initiative industry's bankroll now dwarfs that of the candidates." *San Francisco Chronicle.* May 19, 1998.

Holtz, Debra Levi. "Berkeley Residents Can Take Action on Internet." *San Francisco Chronicle.* Feb. 22, 2000.

Jackson, Maggie. Associated Press. "Most Firms Spy on Employees, Survey Finds." *San Francisco Chronicle*. May 23, 1997.

Jacobs, Jane. *Systems of Survival: A Dialogue on the Moral Foundations of Commerce and the State*. New York: Random House. 1994.

Johnston, David. *The Rhetoric of Leviathan: Thomas Hobbes and the Politics of Cultural Transformation*. Princeton: Princeton University Press. 1986.

Jung, Carl G. *Man and His Symbols*. New York: Bantam Doubleday. 1964.

Kane, Mary. *Newhouse News Service*. "Employers Test Limits of Workplace Privacy." San Francisco Examiner. January 4, 1992.

Katch, M. Ethan. *The Electronic Media and the Transformation of Law*. Oxford: Oxford University Press. 1991.

Kershner, Vlae. "Democracy Gone Awry: Explosion of initiatives lets voters, not elected leaders, steer the state." *San Francisco Chronicle*. May 18. 1998.

--- . "Flaws in Intiative Process Could take Initiative to Fix: Reforms may be on ballot in year 2000." *San Francisco Chronicle*. May 21, 1998.

Keynes, John Maynard. *The General Theory of Employment, Interest and Money*. London: Macmillan. 1936.

Kohlberg, Lawrence. *The Philosophy of Moral Development: Moral States and the Idea of Justice*. New York: Harper & Row. 1981.

Lapham, Lewis H. *Money and Class in America: Notes and Observations on Our Civil Religion*. New York: Weidenfeld & Nicolson. 1988.

Lazarus, David. "PG&E Posts Worst Loss In Firm's History," *San Francisco Chronicle*. April 17, 2001.

Leavitt, Harold J. *Management Psychology*. Third Edition. Chicago: University of Chicago Press. 1975.

Levinson, Daniel J. *The Seasons of a Woman's Life*. New York: Ballentine Books. 1996.

Livy. *The Early History of Rome*. New York: Penguin. 1960.

Lohr, Steve. New York Times. "Poland's Plan--Everyone Becomes a Stockholder." *San Francisco Chronicle*. June 28, 1991.

Lucas, Greg. "Initiative System Popular In Poll: Californians say they like voting directly on state laws." *San Francisco Chronicle*. November 3, 1997.

---. "Not All Votes Are Created Equal," *San Francisco Chronicle*. May 9, 1999.

Machiavelli, Niccolo. *The Prince*. Translated by Hill Thompson. New York: The Heritage Press. 1954.

Maital, Shlomo, and Maital, Sharone L. *Economic Games People Play*. New York: Basic Books. 1984.

Malone, Dumas. *Jefferson and the Rights of Man*. New York: Little, Brown. 1951.

Mansbridge, Jane J. *Beyond Adversary Democracy*. Chicago: University of Chicago Press. 1983.

Marus, George E. And Hanson, Russell L. Eds. *Reconsidering the Democratic Public*. University Park, Penn.: The Pennsylvania State University Press. 1993.

McGrath, William B. *The Heart Does Not Speak English*. Phoenix: O'Sullivan Woodside & Co./Camelback Hospital. 1975.

McLeod, Ramon G. "CEOs Being Rewarded for Dropping the Ax." *San Francisco Chronicle*. May 1, 1997.

Mill, John Stuart. *Three Essays: On Liberty, Representative Government, The Subjection of Women*. Oxford: Oxford University Press. 1975.

Morgan, Edmund S. *Inventing the People: The Rise of Popular Sovereignty in England and America*. New York: W. W. Norton & Co. 1988.

Morris, Regan. Associated Press. "Singapore Rules by E-Government." San Francisco Chronicle. December 12, 2000.

Mount, Ferdinand. *The Subversive Family: An Alternative History of Love and Marriage*. New York: The Free Press. 1992.

Naisbitt, John. *Megatrends*. New York: Warner Books. 1982.

Nozick, Robert. *Anarchy, State, and Utopia*. New York: Basic Books. 1974.

O'Neill, Michael J. *The Roar of the Crowd: How Television and People Power Are Changing the World*. New York: Times Books/Random House. 1993.

Paine, Thomas. *Common Sense*. London: Penguin Books. [1776] 1986.

Parfit, Derek. *Reasons and Persons*. Oxford: Clarendon Press. 1984.

Peterson, Donald E. And Hillkirk, John. *A Better Idea: Redefining the Way Americans Work*. Houghton Mifflin Company. 1991.

Plato. *The Republic*. New York: Penguin. 1974.

Posner, Richard A. *The Problems of Jurisprudence*. Cambridge: Harvard University Press. 1990.

Putnam, Robert D. *Bowling Alone: The Collapse and Revival of American Community*. New York: Simon and Schuster. 1999.

Reuters. "U.S. Treasury Auction Flops: New rules get blame." *San Francisco Chronicle*. November 6, 1991.

Rosenberg, Nathan and Birdzell, L.E. *How the West Grew Rich: The Economic Transformation of the Industrial World*. New York: Basic Books. 1986.

Rousseau, Jean-Jacques. *A Discourse On Inequality*. Trans. by Maurice Cranston. Middlesex, England: Penguin. 1984.

--- . *The Social Contract*. New York: Hafner Publishing Co. 1947.

---. *Emile*. New York: Basic Books. 1979.

Ryan, Michael. "A Recipe for Prosperity." *Parade* magazine. August 17, 1997.

Sagan, Eli. *At the Dawn of Tyranny: The Origins of Individualism, Political Oppression, and the State*. New York: Knopf. 1986.

Sahagun, Louis. "Arizona Governor Convicted: He leaves office today, faces years in prison for fraud." *San Francisco Chronicle*. Sept. 4, 1997.

Sandel, Michael J. *Democracy's Discontent: America in Search of a Public Philosophy*. Cambridge, Mass.: The Belknap Press/Harvard University Press. 1996.

San Jose Mercury News. "Consultant Targets CEO Salaries." *Marin Independent Journal*. December 30, 1992.

Sietsma, Tom. "Ready, Aim, Boycott: media-savvy boycotters find that high-pressure tactics can force corporate change." *San Francisco Chronicle*. February 24, 1993.

Sizer, Theodore. *Horace's School: Redesigning the American High School.* New York: Houghton Mifflin. 1991.

Smith, Hedrick. *The New Russians.* New York: Random House. 1992.

Sowell, Thomas. *A Conflict of Visions.* New York: Morrow. 1987.

Spence, Gerry. *With Justice for None: Destroying an American Myth.* New York: New York Times Books. 1989.

Tiger, Lionel. *The Manufacture of Evil: Ethics, Evolution, and the Industrial System.* New York: Harper & Row. 1987.

Turque, Bill, et. Al. "Wiring Up the Age of Technopolitics." *Newsweek.* June 15, 1992.

Unger, Roberto Mangabeira. *The Critical Legal Studies Movement.* Cambridge, Mass.: Harvard University Press. 1983.

Vogel, David. *Fluctuating Fortunes: The Political Power of Business in America.* New York: Basic Books. 1989.

Weart, Spencer R. *Never at War: Why Democracies Will Not Fight One Another.* New Haven: Yale University Press.

Westbrook, Robert B. *John Dewey and American Democracy.* New York: Cornell University Press. 1992.

Wildermuth, John. "1911 Reform Was meant to Give Citizens More of a Say." *San Francisco Chronicle.* May 18, 1998.

Williams, Lance. "Mayor's aides tapped tenants for 49er votes." *San Francisco Chronicle.* December 28, 1997.

Wilson, James Q. *The Moral Sense.* New York: The Free Press. 1993.

Wright, Robin. "The Leadership Revolution." *Los Angeles Times.* January 19, 1993.

Wuthnow, Robert. *Sharing the Journey: Support Groups and America's New Quest for Community.* New York: The Free Press. 1994.

Yardley, Jim; Barboza, David; and Van Natta, Don. *New York Times* "Lay's political savvy backfires: Insider status now under scrutiny," *San Francisco Chronicle*, February 3, 2002.

Zahn-Waxler, Carolyn; Radke-Yarrow, Marian; and King, Robert A.. "Child Rearing and Children's Prosocial Initiations Toward Victims of Distress." *Child Development 50.* 1979.

INDEX

Abramson, Jeffrey, 119-120

accommodation: between guardians and dependents, 11; between regime of capital and regime of politics, 15

Ackerman, Bruce, 156

Adler, Stephen, 121

affinity groups: purpose of, 70; examples of and effect on democratic learning, 110-111; as tools of polyarchy, 118

Alcaly, Roger E., 127-128

Aristotle, 13; *societas* and *civitas*, 13

Asimov, Nanette, 77, 134

AT&T: breakup of, 58

autonomy: personal and shared, viii-ix; culture than encourages, 66; and collaboration, 69; aptitude and ability, 102; shared, 105; arrested by bureaucratic individualism, 112

Aversa, Jeannine, 147

Bailyn, Bernard, 71

Barabak, Mark Z., 126

Barber, Benjamin, 102-103; on "aristocracy of everyone," 104; contrasting classroom and life experience, 106; on polyarchy, 118-119; and national initiative system, 157